D0072638

DATE DUE

NOV 0 8 2007	
APR 2 9 2008	
APR 2 7 2010	
JUN 1 8 2012	

BRODART, CO.   Cat. No. 23-221-003

Harry S. Truman

and the Cold War Revisionists

HARRY S

Harry S. Truman
and the Cold War Revisionists

Robert H. Ferrell

University of Missouri Press
Columbia and London

Copyright © 2006 by
The Curators of the University of Missouri
University of Missouri Press, Columbia, Missouri 65201
Printed and bound in the United States of America

5 4 3 2 1   10 09 08 07 06

Library of Congress Cataloging-in-Publication Data

Ferrell, Robert H.
   Harry S. Truman and the Cold War revisionists / Robert H. Ferrell.
     p.   cm.
   Summary: "Ferrell argues that revisionists are often hasty and argumentative in their judgments, understanding neither the times nor the players. These essays challenge the revisionists' perception of President Harry Truman by going below surface appearances of history to examine how this presidency actually functioned in response to unprecedented problems and crises"—Provided by publisher.
   Includes bibliographical references and index.
   ISBN-13: 978-0-8262-1653-3 (hard cover : alk. paper)
   ISBN-10: 0-8262-1653-6 (hard cover : alk. paper)
   1. Truman, Harry S., 1884–1972.   2. United States—History—1945–1953. 3. United States—Foreign relations—1945–1953.   4. Cold War.   5. Political culture—United States—History—20th century.   6. United States—History— 1945–1953—Historiography.   7. United States—Foreign relations—1945–1953— Historiography.   I. Title.
   E813.F47   2006
   973.918—dc22   2005036668

Designer: Jennifer Cropp
Typesetter: Phoenix Type, Inc.
Printer and binder: The Maple-Vail Book Manufacturing Group
Typefaces: Minion and Bodoni

*Publication of this book has been generously
assisted by a contribution from Sprint Foundation.*

CONTENTS

PREFACE

Every now and then a notion or idea arises that is radically wrong. Such was the case when years ago a large group of historians and political scientists known as revisionists undertook to criticize the foreign policy of President Harry S. Truman. The group flourished in the late 1960s and early 1970s. Its adherents saw Truman as the originator of the troubles between the United States and Russia, the cold war that began after World War II and lasted until the collapse of the Soviet Union in 1991.

There is nothing wrong, let me add hastily, with the notion or idea of revisionism, taken by itself. My generation of historians, who began their studies in the years just after the war of 1941–1945, read and appreciated the essays of the best-known historian of the time, Charles A. Beard, who declared that revision was the essence of scholarship. We were fascinated by the similar wisdom of Carl L. Becker of Cornell University, who spoke of "every man his own historian," showing how out of a desire to learn about the past we all change our memory if it proves faulty. We are all revisionists.

But the cold war revisionists who attacked President Truman did not understand the time in which he was president nor the man himself. They did not believe that after entrance of the United States into World

War II there had to be a sea change in American foreign policy—the country no longer could follow the wisdom of President George Washington and remain apart from the world, intervening only to change the wicked ways of Europe and, in 1941–1945, of East Asia. They did not appreciate the postwar military weakness of the country, both in conventional and in nuclear arms; the American nation possessed a near totally ineffective army and had neither sufficient nuclear weapons nor the means to deliver them. If anything the revisionists, myopic to a fault, believed the American arsenal, conventional and nuclear, was too strong, that it threatened the Soviet Union. Similarly the revisionists misestimated the man they considered the mastermind of the cold war. They did not see that he was one of the most clearheaded, farsighted presidents ever to occupy the office of chief executive of the United States. He possessed an ability to stand away from his own feelings, to subtract his personality from whatever he was contemplating, to consult only the need to ensure the future of the Republic. When he changed the foreign policy of his country in a series of great measures in 1947–1949, and took the country into a war in Korea the next year that continued until the end of his presidency and beyond, he did it for the good of the country and of the nation's friends abroad. It was an altogether remarkable presidency, and the essays that follow seek to point that out.

I have felt some hesitation in writing about scholarly friends who would like to forget their lapses of years ago. The decades have passed, and my friend of that earlier time, William A. Williams, has now passssed on; I always admired him personally, and it is difficult to criticize him. Another good friend has had trouble with eyesight, no longer able to read as he would wish, and it is saddening to think of his present-day plight. One can only say that the larger task is to help set the record straight. In that regard, and I confess it, I celebrate the president from Independence, Missouri. Readers of the following chapters may notice this enthusiasm.

Acknowledgments

I do wish to thank my friend of many years, Lawrence S. Kaplan, for assistance with several of the essays that follow; we have known each other ever since we encountered the rules of a certain graduate school. My thanks to Sadao Asada, George M. Elsey, D. M. Giangreco, John Lukacs, Robert J. Maddox, Robert P. Newman, and Steven L. Rearden. Similarly to Randy Sowell, archivist, and Elizabeth Safly, librarian, of the Harry S. Truman Library, and to Mitchell A. Yockelson of the National Archives. The anonymous readers for the University of Missouri Press, in particular Richard S. Kirkendall, were helpful indeed. Again, I so appreciate the enthusiasm of the director and editor-in-chief of the University of Missouri Press, Beverly Jarrett, and the shrewd judgment of the managing editor, Jane Lago. Carolyn and Lorin were of large help, as always, and I look forward to a third helper they will soon make available.

HARRY S. TRUMAN

and the Cold War Revisionists

ONE

Revisionism

In the early 1960s a well-known student of American history, the late John L. Snell, published an article in the *American Historical Review* in which he dealt with several books on the origins of the cold war; after criticizing two of them severely, he urged historians to turn their attention to that part of the recent past and write about it in the best traditions of their discipline.[1] He could not have known then that in the next few years some able historians, just out of graduate school, together with a young student of English literature, a disillusioned foreign service officer, a linguist, and other interested individuals would radically reverse the views Snell and his contemporaries had advanced about American-Russian relations in 1945. Soon there would be a sizable literature on the origins of the cold war that would find enthusiastic acceptance among college and university students throughout the country. It would describe Snell and his aging colleagues as traditionalists, their historical opinions as received truths, and their conclusions as cold war rhetoric.

Consider the ideas about the origins of the cold war that were being proposed in the early 1970s. How different they were from the views of a decade earlier! So-called revisionist historians were writing that President Franklin D. Roosevelt's subtle treatment of the Soviet Union had been reversed by his successor, Harry S. Truman, who saw foreign affairs as a checker game instead of the chess game it really is; that the United States under Truman's direction had tried to oust the Soviet Union from Eastern Europe, giving little or no consideration to Russia's security needs in an area close to its borders; that the Americans had dropped two atomic bombs on the Japanese in order to alert the Russians to U.S. power; that the government had striven to keep the Russians aware of the Americans' monopoly of atomic power and, largely for such a purpose, advanced a system of international control of atomic weapons—the Baruch Plan—that was almost bound to fail. Meanwhile, the United States government had used every economic device at hand, such as cutting off lend-lease to the USSR, reneging on the reparations agreements concluded at the end of the war, and refusing to consider seriously the Russians' pressing need for a postwar loan. Then, early in 1946, the Americans had seized upon an admitted Soviet reluctance to get out of northern Iran and, in a confrontation at the United Nations, virtually forced the Russians out. The next year, 1947, had marked a rapid increase in American-Russian antagonism, for President Truman intervened in the Greek civil war with the Truman Doctrine and in order to gain support scared hell out of the country, to use a phrase attributed to Sen. Arthur H. Vandenberg. (Somewhat later, beginning in 1950, the administration would get what it deserved for this tactic, at the hands of a senator who took a free ride on the anticommunist bandwagon.) The Truman Doctrine inspired the administration to sponsor the Marshall Plan, a program worthy in itself but which had the unfortunate effect of dividing Europe; the president, the revisionists believed, probably had this divisive effect in mind, for in his memoirs he described the Truman Doctrine and Marshall Plan as being two halves of the same walnut. All the while, through a series of moves, the administration was creating a new state in Europe, West Germany, for the purpose of enlisting German industry and eventually a German army to protect the free world against world communism. By the early 1970s the revisionists had begun to turn attention to the nation's postwar policies in the Far

East and were reexamining the origins of the Korean War; the outbreak of that conflict, they believed, was at least in part attributable to the policies of the United States.

1

The new historical views of the cold war were fascinating interpretations, and in seeking to understand how such a literature could arise, the inquiring observer notices, first of all, the relative youth of the interpreters. The authors of the revisionist books and articles were young men who remembered little or nothing about World War II. Lloyd C. Gardner, later professor of history and chairman of the department at Rutgers, had no thoughts about a career in history in 1939, when he was five years old. Barton J. Bernstein was born in 1936, Gar Alperovitz in 1937, and David J. Horowitz in 1939. It is possible to list the ages of other revisionists as well, such as that of the later foreign service officer and journalist—and a markedly good one—Ronald Steel, born in 1934. It is true that the teacher of some of the leading revisionists, a charismatic figure who inspired them to adopt his own "open door" approach to their historical judgments, William A. Williams, was an adult in 1939, a first-year student at the United States Naval Academy. The point remains that most of the revisionists could not have remembered much if anything about World War II, the beginning of the cold war, and even the Korean War. They came of age in the middle and late 1950s and shortly thereafter were in graduate school preparing to enter the teaching profession in colleges and universities.

At risk of seeming unduly analytical about a group of young men as fascinating as their interpretations—individuals who were good, sharp writers, who had a way of cutting quickly to their point or points, who must all have been fine lecturers and impressive seminar teachers—one should venture to suggest another factor in their professional growth. They came into the teaching profession in a heady decade when the student population was tripling, faculties were tripling, grants were easy to come by, and books easy to publish. Indeed, anyone with brains and

ambition could attain the titles of doctor and professor in a phenome-
nally short time, with quite a decent salary and the prospects of quick
promotions and more salary.

And always there was that generation gap, the feeling that the older
scholars—not so old, the oldsters themselves might have thought, but
it made no difference what they thought—were, if not over the hill, then
intellectually trapped in fantasies about World War II and what they
believed had happened afterward. They were judged able to think of
few international influences other than Hitler, Munich, the Nazi-Soviet
Pact, the long war, and especially the Russians' refusal of friendship after
the fighting. This older generation had written the textbooks and the
monographs and was in control of the departments and the deanships,
and it could not get Hitler out of its thinking. Its contemporaries were
running the federal government and dominating foreign policy. The
young men who came into the teaching profession in the early 1960s
viewed this scene with the impatience of all young men, an impatience
in fair part generated by the fact of youth—their having been too young
to have made many mistakes or to have known deep disappointment—
and by the fact that they came to manhood at a time when the draft
calls for the U.S. Army were small because no large war was being waged,
or even a police action like Korea, so their careers were not blighted or
interrupted by military service. Having come to their own stations of
life without interruption, they considered the preceding generation to
be a fountainhead of stupidity:

> Our elders seem mired in the dead past: the Depression, the War, and
> the competition with Russia. The Second World War, which most of us
> are too young to remember except through the movies, was the last war
> that conceivably could be defined as just. What followed the defeat of
> Germany and Japan was a series of dynastic struggles between the new
> superpowers. Korea, like Vietnam, now seems like just another imperial
> war for spheres of influence, and the cold war itself little more than a
> power contest between rival empires, both prevented from launching a
> full-scale war from fear of suffering instant obliteration. Can there be
> anybody under forty who sincerely believes in the morality of American
> foreign policy, or that such a word is relevant to any nation's diplomacy?[2]

One should perhaps explain at this point that the older generation was not charmed by the cold war revisionists. But behind their hurt feelings, these critics of the cold war revisionists constantly wondered why the new left writers (as some of them described themselves) adopted one special interpretation of U.S. foreign policy, the Williams interpretation about the open door. The generation gap may have been responsible; for the most part the older generation could not believe in absolutes. Whatever the reason, the majority of older historians were incredulous as they observed the easy way in which the revisionists picked up the favorite thesis of Williams and used it as a basis for their writings. One of their impulses for using the thesis was understandable. Walter LaFeber and Lloyd Gardner had been trained at the University of Wisconsin and were Williams's students. It is difficult to understand why at Wisconsin, where a half century earlier Frederick Jackson Turner had taught about the importance of the frontier in the development of the nation, Williams was able to capture so much attention for another monocausal interpretation. I recall keenly the first time I heard this interpretation from Williams himself in the mid-1950s—during a little seminar for historians conducted by George L. Anderson at the University of Kansas. Williams gave a paper showing how the open door policy was naught but an extension of Turner's old frontier thesis, and how hope for an open door for American commerce had dominated U.S. foreign policy since the 1890s, if not earlier. I was chosen to respond first to the paper and could only express my simpleminded wonder that such an all-encompassing thesis should be developed, considering that the author's generation had been brought up on a historical diet of the essays of Beard and Becker, which taught that historical truths are relative.

Whatever one might think of the datedness of one-cause history, the revisionists almost without exception espoused the open door theory of U.S. foreign policy and in books and articles pushed the theory for all the traffic would bear, and a good deal more. LaFeber's doctoral thesis, entitled "The New Empire," a survey of U.S. foreign policy from 1860 until 1898, quickly published, concluded that a search for raw materials and markets was the dominant force of the time.[3] Gardner's thesis, also published and also soon available in a paperback edition, came very close to saying that in the 1930s the effort to push a diplomacy of U.S. commerce, the open door for U.S. products, led to a clash with the Axis powers and eventually war.[4] As Irwin Unger said, how much more easily could the younger generation have hoped to tangle with the older than to assert that the war against Hitler was only a war for American markets?[5] LaFeber and Gardner passed from their doctoral theses into analyses of the cold war, using the Williams principle. They not merely gathered around their arguments against U.S. management of the cold war an old-fashioned aura of the open door (everyone knew, of course, that the open door policy failed in China when tried at the turn of the century), but they also pointed out that such a recent piece of journalism as Henry Luce's 1941 "American Century" editorial in *Life* magazine was only a reassertion of the open door. According to LaFeber, in the post-1945 years the U.S. open door policy toward trade and politics in Eastern Europe clashed with the USSR's desire for security around its borders. The then young military historian Stephen E. Ambrose slipped into cold war revisionism and wrote agreeably that the policy of containment of Russia "was never more than a euphemism for the expansion of American influence and dominance."[6]

Perhaps the revisionists' fascination with the Williams theory of the open door, a belief that American commercial expansion was the root cause of the cold war as of other discreditable episodes in the nation's history, derived from the politics of several of the revisionists. Williams and Gardner were socialists, and so were Horowitz and Gabriel Kolko; the latter two subjected their readers to heavy doses of socialism. Kolko was constantly talking about the necessary preconditions of this event or that, and the preconditions were almost always economic.

The fallaciousness of such an approach as the open door was often pointed out, but the explanations evidently were not convincing. The winner of the Pulitzer Prize for history in 1972, Carl Degler, in a review of Williams's latest book showed the improbability of an economic cause for the Spanish-American War of 1898, which Williams attributed in fair part to the desire of American farmers to expand their markets.[7] If the farmers wanted markets, Degler countered, that desire might explain their support of the war, but how about the city folk who, if the farmers had been denied foreign markets, would have had cheaper food because of overproduction at home? What did they have to gain by supporting the farmers? Williams, Gardner, and other revisionists—good socialists—were bothered, indeed haunted, by capitalism, a kind of bogey. Were they not sophisticated enough as students of American history to know that if there ever was a predatory, power-seeking era, an unabashedly exploitive period when the capitalists prowled through the cottages of the proletariat like wolves, that time had long since passed? As for U.S. goals in World War II, John L. Gaddis in a paper at a Boston meeting of the American Historical Association in 1970 showed that economics could not possibly explain the U.S. motives in fighting the Axis powers:

> Public and private statements made by policymakers at the time . . . indicate that they did not accord the open door the importance revisionist historians have given it. President Roosevelt and his advisers did place great emphasis on reviving a multilateral system of world trade, but this was only one element of a larger scheme for avoiding future wars, influenced primarily by a determination to avoid the mistakes of World War I and the interwar period. Washington officials articulated with at least equal emphasis such other goals as unconditional surrender, the disarmament of defeated enemies, self-determination, and the establishment of a new collective security organization.[8]

Carried to its logical conclusion, the revisionist economic interpretation indicated, of course, that the cold war was an unavoidable conflict, a clash for which individuals could bear no responsibility. But then the revisionists wobbled on their one-cause interpretation and spent much analysis on how certain individuals, had they been listened to, could have changed history.[9]

Might it not be that the concern of the revisionists with their open door theory showed that they were bothered by the enormous international, domestic, political, economic, and social transformations during the 1960s and the decades prior to it—changes that many of the revisionists did not like and for which they were seeking a satisfying explanation? In an article Arthur M. Schlesinger Jr. pointed out how, in the course of the changes of a quarter century, the individual often found himself in the hands of a kind of soulless, uncontrollable organization, and rather than seeking to control change so as to allow for the continuing movement of the individual will, many people railed against change or attributed it to some single, simple cause when, in fact, it was due to the interaction in almost cosmic proportions of a vast complex of ideas and interests. "The basic task," as Schlesinger proposed it, was not to ride off to tilt against some windmill, but "to control and humanize the forces of change in order to prevent them from tearing our society apart."[10]

But all this discussion of what was at the center of revisionist thought about the cold war or what might have been at the center is to say nothing about the scholarly techniques of revisionist writers—about which something needs to be remarked in general before turning to specific points of revision and how the revisionists sought to prove them. Here one came to the issue, then much discussed, of a usable past. Let no reader hesitate to accuse the cold war revisionists of taking the present into the past. And in the course of observing their uses of the past it was not necessary to agree with Unger (who saw a good deal of historical revision as an effort to domesticate American radicalism) in order to conclude that cold war revisionists were not very tidy in their methods. Adam Ulam wrote an injunction about historical scholarship that the revisionists would have done well to take to heart; the historian, Ulam said, must accept the past as he finds it:

> Before he becomes a philosopher of history or a judge, he must tell us what actually happened. His primary duty is not to be attuned to the currently fashionable trends in public thinking or to be a counselor to statesmen. It is to ascertain what, in terms of our knowledge, is a fact, what could be a reasonable hypothesis, and what must remain a conjecture. If he does not meet that test, he is a moralist or a publicist but not an historian.[11]

The cold war revisionists surely fell into several errors of historical method. For one, whatever their view of U.S. responsibility for the cold war, the revisionists adopted an unhistorical—and also unfair—tactic by virtually assuming that a statesman was wrong until proved right. Anglo-Saxon jurisprudence holds the opposite view. Most historians would assert that such a presumption about the nation's leaders has not squared with the record of, now, two hundred and more years. Should historians then conclude that the era after 1945 was a sudden throwback, not to American practice, but to the statecraft of Renaissance Italy?

The revisionists also were expert in using some of the old ploys of writers who attempt to make points, as when they tried to slip arguments in on the unsuspecting reader. It was amusing to observe the virtuoso performances, up and down the literary keyboard, of Barton J. Bernstein, who could write, "A year before the global crusade of the Truman Doctrine . . ." to introduce his account of an event. In similar manner he managed to bring into sudden focus a highly dubious point made by Gar Alperovitz (that the United States dropped two atomic bombs on Japan to impress the Russians) and assert it as truth: "In 1945, when the United States sought to liberate Eastern Europe with 'atomic diplomacy,' Lippmann subtly warned . . . ," and again: "[The journalist Walter Lippmann] did not know that Secretary Byrnes had already tried to use atomic diplomacy to frighten the Soviets out of Eastern Europe."[12] In a small meeting that I attended at the Truman Library in Independence, Missouri, the assembled scholars were treated to a bland assumption of the Alperovitz thesis by Bernstein; when challenged on the subject he answered, "I thought everyone agreed with Alperovitz." Similar examples of one-upmanship appeared in the writings of another revisionist, Gardner, who among other tricks juxtaposed two irrelevant facts: "Even before Bullitt's note arrived in the White House, the President had acted."[13]

Gardner's essay on William C. Bullitt in *Architects of Illusion* was a masterly example of how to influence readers—a combination of fact and surmise, a kind of glancing commentary about the era of Bullitt, based on the assumption that the U.S. ambassador to Russia and to France during the 1930s represented some large body of American opinion. In truth, Bullitt was one of the oddest ducks ever to inhabit any duck run of foreign policy, a most quixotic individual who, contrary to the innuendo in Gardner's essay, had almost no influence on Roosevelt by the time FDR began to think about the country's entrance into war, not to mention in later years when "Bill" Bullitt was painfully isolated from influence on anyone except, possibly, Henry Luce.[14]

John Gimbel, the author of a much-cited study of the U.S. occupation of Germany, complained at length about "the kind of hocus-pocus that is often passed off as historical research by those who write cold-war history," and this prestidigitation was sometimes observable in the summoning of nonexperts to give expert—that is, convenient—explanations.[15] LaFeber's revisionist *America, Russia, and the Cold War* made much out of a letter from Alfred P. Sloan to Bernard Baruch, written in 1945, that LaFeber found in the Baruch papers at Princeton. Sloan wanted the American government to revive German industry, contrary to the joint chiefs of staff paper numbered 1067, which was supposed to guide American military governors. Yet Sloan's view of what should be postwar policy toward Germany was Sloan's view, and whether it figured in the calculus of the U.S. Government must at the least be suspect. The letter did play into the beliefs of many students who were sure that General Motors was up to monkey business.[16]

David Donald, in what for the most part was an attack on cold war revisionism, praised the books of Kolko and LaFeber, saying that these revisionist authors and not the older scholars of the establishment "have written the basic books, resting upon massive research, on the last three decades of our foreign relations."[17] Donald was an expert on the American Civil War and on Reconstruction, the Pulitzer Prize biographer of Charles Sumner, but he was dead wrong about cold war revisionism, for he obviously had not checked out the revisionists' footnotes. Much of their footnoting was as defective as Charles C. Tansill's documentation about the coming of war with Japan.[18] As Tansill documented the irrelevant and the well known, so Kolko and LaFeber produced an array of footnotes that appeared significant. But underneath those awesome citations could be a remarkable thinness. How otherwise explain the constant appearance in LaFeber's text on the origins of the cold war of citations to the unpublished Baruch papers at Princeton? Most writers about the post-1945 period—and surely a majority of the individuals who took part in the politics of the era—knew that Baruch was a vain, pompous, egotistical self-advertiser who, by his own recounting, had made a fortune in the stock market. His opinions were grossly unrepresentative, but he occasionally had to be brought in on political issues because his conservative politics tended to scare away Republican and crackpot critics.[19] LaFeber knew these facts, but the Baruch papers happened to be open and were full of opinions, a convenient quarry from which to mine commentaries, such as the letter from Sloan about free enterprise in Germany. Responsible historians, one might conclude, should not use the memorabilia of "old goats," a label Truman pinned on Baruch. Much of the other documentation by revisionists recycled the commentaries of critics of policy, such as Lippmann, Henry A. Wallace, Claude Pepper, Glen Taylor, or James A. Warburg, who always were operating on the outside of affairs and whose opinions were so flighty that no sensible statesman could have welcomed them into the inner councils of power.[20]

To add another detail to the above points about documentation, one should not fail to notice how the revisionists loved to cite the works of each other. Alperovitz, in a footnote for his paperback of collected essays, recommended LaFeber's *America, Russia, and the Cold War* as "the best brief one-volume survey of the postwar period"; it could be "usefully supplemented" by Richard J. Barnet's *Intervention and Revolution: America's Confrontation with Insurgent Movements around the World.* Both, he stated, "are excellent, especially for college teaching." Gardner, in his *Architects of Illusion,* found his good friend LaFeber's *America, Russia, and the Cold War* an "excellent survey" and remarked his "indebtedness to Professor LaFeber." LaFeber's subsequently published *Origins of the Cold War,* a book of documents and pseudo documents (he included the Sloan letter), credited Gardner's *Economic Aspects of New Deal Diplomacy* as "the best synthesis of the entire 1933–1945 period" and stated that *Architects of Illusion* "is the best work covering the entire 1940s."[21]

In regard to documentation, Gaddis in the preface to his very able nonrevisionist study, *The United States and the Origins of the Cold War, 1941–1947,* cautioned historians of the era after 1945 to remember that they were dealing almost entirely with American materials. Scholars, he said, faced a peculiar problem in that "we have little reliable information about what went on inside the Kremlin during the same period."[22] Unless they could gain access to the information about Russian activities and thought of the time, they had to write with something less than dogmatism.

Speaking of the American side, I comment on the fact—not well understood even within the historical profession, much less among the public at large—that cold war revisionists and other scholars interested in our foreign policy following World War II used government archival materials to only slight extent because almost all of these materials then were closed. In 1973, the high point of revisionism, the State Department's archives had just become available for events through the year 1947. Access to the archives of the Department of State was tied to publication of annual volumes in the documentary series *Foreign Relations of the United States.* The eminent diplomatic historian Dexter Perkins, eighty-four years old at that time, a past president of the American Historical Association, author of twenty-three books, most of them about American foreign policy, in a communication to the newsletter of the American Historical Association cautioned his young colleagues, the revisionists, in a pointed manner. "There are . . . reasons," he wrote, "for great modesty in dogmatizing about the history of American foreign policy in the last quarter century. The documentation is incomplete."[23] How could Donald say that some of the revisionists produced the basic books, resting upon massive research, when for the most part they had not even had the benefit of published volumes in the *Foreign Relations* series, not to mention the mountain of documentation that lay behind *Foreign Relations?*[24]

The size of the American unpublished records leads to a final observation about the methods of the cold war revisionists, although this observation was only indirectly related to the State Department files in Washington. It concerned generally the mass of material, unpublished and published, that a researcher finds available. The heterogeneous, huge body of documentation made the historian of the cold war, revisionist or traditionalist, long for the task of the scholar of the middle ages who, in confronting a problem of documentation, may need to deal with three documents, two of which are fakes (his task being to determine which is the original). Any researcher on the cold war, even if he delved into the huge body of material that lay outside the State Department archives, had to, if he was looking for some meaning amid the near chaos, fix upon two or three or four principles and from them try to derive some overreaching theme or thesis by which, at least in his own mind, he could order the material. Otherwise, he could spend a lifetime behind the paper barricades. But the revisionist perhaps refused to change his thesis when contrary evidence appeared. If he felt strongly that Vietnam was not a great error but only the most recent collapse in a row of dominoes, he would tend to believe that—to use Kolko's Marxist phrase—the necessary preconditions were there and hence the thesis could not be wrong, despite the evidence. At such a point the trap of the present would close, not with a bang but ever so softly, over the would-be student of the past.

2

In analyzing the revisionist view of the cold war in some detail it is necessary to say at the outset that there was no accepted body of revisionist doctrine, that the loose aggregation of young scholars, a few older scholars, and some journalists who received the name of revisionists did not agree even upon the name, which to some of them was a foolish term. There were very considerable disagreements in regard to the origins of the cold war; no simple listing of revisionist views can do justice to individual, dissenting members of the group. Even so, there were generally held theories and hypotheses.

For the first year of the cold war, 1945, the revisionists advanced three theories, the initial one of which was that President Roosevelt was a subtle, sophisticated operator in foreign relations as in domestic politics, and that President Truman was pretty much the opposite; hence, for a personal reason alone, the change in the presidency, U.S. foreign relations took a downward plunge, once the feisty, hard-hitting Missouri politician became president. Gardner was not, apparently, sure of this argument, although it was perhaps in another particular that he spoke of a devil theory of history. Kolko cavalierly brushed this personal argument aside and accused some of the revisionists of being enamored with personalities in history, instead of being concerned with forces, the latter of which, according to Kolko, were the determinants in the inexorable movement of capitalism toward its Waterloo. Whatever the dissenting opinions, there did seem to be a belief on the part of most revisionists that Truman stiffened up U.S. diplomacy to such an extent that he may have reversed it. Athan G. Theoharis, who was concerned about the effect of foreign policy in bringing on the McCarthyist excesses, was convinced that Truman's new outlook was of major importance.[25]

Thomas G. Paterson and Les Adler, in one of the explanations of their rambunctious article on "red fascism," asserted that Truman "was clearly more blustering, less cautious, and less willing to compromise."[26] This view, one might add, echoed the contemporary opinion of many New Deal Democrats who, for a while after the war, moved toward support of Henry Wallace; at the outset of the Truman presidency these liberals believed that the country's leader from Missouri was junking FDR's foreign policies, just as he was abandoning the Roosevelt heritage in domestic politics.[27] The usual demonstration of Truman's tough attitude toward the Russians was to point to his treatment of Vyacheslav M. Molotov when the Soviet foreign minister passed through Washington in April 1945, en route to the San Francisco Conference of the United Nations.[28]

It is an interesting speculation to think of one leader reversing the policy of his predecessor, and Schlesinger has pointed out the dramatic temptation here, yet this theory about a change in policies had less to it than met the eye.[29] Roosevelt was a compromiser, sometimes to the point of dissimulation. At other times he could be so devious or so unable to communicate his purposes that to the present day one is uncertain what he originally had in mind, if anything. An individual with this makeup could drive his straightforward subordinates to distraction or to fury. General George C. Marshall never completely trusted Roosevelt; the only time Marshall went to Hyde Park to see the president, despite many invitations, was on the occasion of Roosevelt's funeral. As compared with Roosevelt, Truman was a breath of fresh air, open and businesslike. All these points have been made many times and are well known, but to push them into a conclusion that Truman, whose modus operandi was so different, sought to reverse Roosevelt's foreign policy is to make a historical mistake.

Truman in 1941 had delivered himself of a snap judgment that Soviet publicists, and the revisionists, would never forget. Shortly after the Germans attacked the Soviet Union he had said that he was delighted and he hoped they would fight each other to the death, with the United States helping whichever side was losing. But this opinion had given way to more maturity of thought long before 1945 and his inheritance of the presidency, and there is every reason to believe that, despite the little talk session with Molotov, the president loyally undertook to carry out the foreign policy of his predecessor. For one circumstance, he was too new in the office to have formed many detailed opinions on foreign policy. For another, he was properly sensitive to the fact that he had been elected vice president only because he was on the ticket with Roosevelt, and it would have been presumptuous of him in April 1945 to start off on his own presidential policies, foreign or domestic. For a third, his actions in the spring of 1945 showed that he wanted to get along with Stalin. Churchill was pressing the new president to act, for the old Briton as well as many members of Roosevelt's disgruntled official family eagerly anticipated a more straightforward presidency. As is well known, the prime minister wanted a showdown with the Russians. To Churchill's intense chagrin, Truman refused to allow American troops to remain in the parts of the Soviet-designated zone of Germany they had entered in the last days of the war against Hitler.[30]

The revisionists liked to show that at the outset of his presidency Truman was listening to some hard-line advisers (to use a later expression). Secretary of War Henry L. Stimson was upset because of the anti-Russian feeling among Truman's advisers, notably Ambassador Averell Harriman and the latter's Moscow assistant in charge of Russian lend-lease, Major General John R. Deane. But Herbert Feis's 1970 book, *From Trust to Terror*, pointed out that, at this time, Harriman was not on the inside of Truman's group of advisers, nor for that matter was Stimson. The new president had turned for advice to FDR's chief of staff, then his own, Admiral William D. Leahy.[31] At the outset Truman's opinions on foreign policy seem to have been so uncertain that at the same time he sent Harry Hopkins to Moscow to assure Stalin of the new administration's desire to cooperate with the Soviets to achieve European peace he dispatched Joseph E. Davies to see Churchill in England. Davies, to be sure, was well known to be "soft" on communism, and he must have impressed Churchill negatively. While he was serving as ambassador to Russia, prior to World War II, Davies had justified the purge trials and in his *Mission to Moscow* described Stalin as no tyrant, a judgment he supported with the statement that a child would sit on the dictator's lap and a dog would sidle up to him.

In trying to demonstrate that Truman took a hard line after Roosevelt's more subtle approach, the revisionists in one respect discovered some fire, or at least some good quotations. In addition to relying for diplomatic advice upon Admiral Leahy, Truman turned to former senator James F. Byrnes, and almost immediately after the end of the San Francisco Conference, when it was possible to ease the hopelessly naive Edward R. Stettinius Jr. out of the secretaryship, he designated the South Carolinian as secretary of state. The arrangement was to propel Stettinius into the United Nations.[32] Byrnes talked tough within administration circles in the summer of 1945, and the revisionists found several good quotations to show that he was no naïf. But contrary to the revisionists, Byrnes's views on Russian-American relations in 1945 are difficult to pin down. Probably he was himself unsure of his position, as was true of most Americans at the time. Underneath his geniality he resented being pushed around. He had the impression—which was as good as true, considering what the Russians were doing in Eastern Europe—that the Soviets were being extremely difficult. But then in the autumn and winter of 1945–1946, Byrnes appears to have weakened toward the Russians to the extent that—so Truman in a famous section of his memoirs was to state—the president was forced to rebuke the secretary of state for "babying" the Soviets. Byrnes denied this allegation, and there is no reason to doubt his denial. The point is that, in Byrnes, the revisionists clearly were dealing with no doctrinaire on the Russian question. How did that fact fit some of their hard-line commentaries about Byrnes's Machiavellian influence on the inexperienced president? Moreover, the Byrnes papers at the Clemson University library opened in 1971, and it would have behooved the revisionists, who wrote at great length abut Byrnes's baneful influence, to take a look at the secretary's private correspondence.

It would be possible to relate in detail the evidence, which is undeniable, that Roosevelt was hardening his own view of the Russians just before his death.[33] It should suffice to say of the contention that Truman reversed Roosevelt's policy that it was at the least unproved and that most signs pointed in the direction of continuity.

In considering the responsibility of leading personalities there seemed much more reason to believe that Stalin, rather than Truman, forced the cold war, though the reasoning for that conclusion was widely open to debate. Perhaps the Jacques Duclos letter of April 1945 was a communist declaration of war on the West, though perhaps it was not.[34] Perhaps Stalin was mad; perhaps he was not, although of his later madness there was excellent testimony by N. S. Khrushchev. As Melvin Croan, a political scientist at the University of Wisconsin, remarked at a scholarly conference in London, the internal compulsions of the Soviet state in 1945—the political unreliability of large sections of the Soviet people, the need to force a rebuilding of Soviet industry after the war's devastation—made it highly convenient, maybe even necessary, for Stalin to have an external enemy, for him to have a cold war.[35] It is clear that nothing short of the conversion of the United States into a satellite would have sufficed to abolish Stalin's distrust. Even that might not have sufficed, considering the manner in which he could assail his closest friends, or states with the friendliest political systems, for some mythical deviation or other.

A second hypothesis of the revisionists concerning diplomacy during the year 1945, on which they showed considerable agreement, was that after the Yalta Conference the United States sought to intervene in Russia's security zone in Eastern Europe, trying to gain influence, perhaps even dominance, over the cordon sanitaire of weak nations lying between Western Europe and the Soviet borders. Henry Wallace was saying in 1946 that the United States was being self-righteous in trying to force its way into supervision of the politics of the Eastern European nations and that Russian "efforts to develop a security zone in Eastern Europe . . . are small change from the point of view of military power as compared with our air bases in Greenland, Okinawa and many other places thousands of miles from our shores." Lippmann soon was pointing to a double standard in that, at the end of the war, the Anglo-Americans had dominated the reorganization of the Italian government. Stalin, in a cable to Truman in 1945, remarked that he had not sought to intervene in the politics of Belgium or Greece. What to the revisionists seemed a proof of the Truman administration's hypocrisy in trying to give the Soviets advice on Eastern Europe was the telephone conversation on May 8, 1945, between Assistant Secretary of War John J. McCloy, present at the San Francisco Conference, and Secretary Stimson, in the course of which these two administration stalwarts agreed that the United States could maintain its sphere of influence in Latin America and still reasonably ask the Soviets for concessions in Eastern Europe; McCloy and Stimson spoke of having their cake and eating it too, a metaphor not soon forgotten by their critics of the 1960s.

The revisionists pointed out that, during the war, President Roosevelt tried to avoid talk of a division of Europe or the world into spheres of influence and favored a kind of universalism that, some of the revisionists said, was nothing less than the open door for American commerce. The revisionists noted that this presidential strategy of delaying decisions about the character of the postwar political map had its special advantage in Eastern Europe, the homeland of large numbers of the Democratic Party's supporters. It is true that Roosevelt at Teheran told Stalin he hoped there would be no decision affecting the map of Eastern Europe until after the 1944 presidential election, and mentioned the Polish problem in particular. There is no question that the strategy of delaying the drawing of postwar boundaries and the establishment of political regimes allowed Roosevelt to avoid telling the American people, especially his Polish American supporters, some hard truths about what the Red Army might do in the regions it occupied. Stalin's outrageous refusal to send the Red Army across the Vistula to assist the Warsaw uprising in 1944 while the Germans blew up the city, block by block, should have carried a message to any American Poles who wondered about the postwar policies of the Soviets. Then, at Yalta, Roosevelt almost openly yielded to the Russians' wishes about boundaries, politics, and human rights in Eastern Europe. When Admiral Leahy protested, FDR said there was nothing the United States could do. He glossed over his inaction by arranging the Yalta Declaration on Liberated Europe, and the revisionists were quite right in pointing out also that the terms for operation of the Allied control councils in the occupied territories gave complete control to Soviet troops.

After his initial angry outburst at Molotov, Truman accepted this state of affairs, as well he might have, the revisionists to the contrary. As the Soviet Union in the next two years committed outrage after outrage in Eastern Europe, the protests that issued from Washington were protests and could be nothing more. The revisionists interpreted them as efforts at interference, failing to understand the president's political problem in dealing with such senators as Vandenberg of Michigan, who represented a large group of Polish American constituents, and failing also to understand the need for any decent human being to speak out against the repression behind the iron curtain. The revisionists, as moral men, spoke out against the war in Vietnam, but they could not understand similar efforts by the United States for the suffering peoples of Eastern Europe. Should one mention again the phrase *double standard*?

Herbert Feis believed in retrospect that the Western allies should have risked a break with Stalin at Yalta rather than make the Eastern European agreements, but the bleakness of the Western position emerges clearly in Feis's estimate of the result in such a case. "I think," he wrote, "that if they had taken that risk, Stalin would have given in slightly about Poland."[36]

What in retrospect strikes one as peculiar about the situation in Eastern Europe is not that the Soviets feared an open door to American trade and therefore erected barriers to American capitalism (it never seems to have bothered them much), nor that the Americans saw Soviet domination as the camel's nose of socialism under the tent of Western Europe (there is not much American official testimony in this regard), nor that the Russians were sensitive about the politics of the states along their borders (undoubtedly this was the case), but that the Soviets found it necessary to make the Eastern European countries utterly subservient to Russian rule. They had for examples their neighbor Finland, a little country that behaved, and Czechoslovakia prior to 1948, which likewise showed care for Soviet sensibilities. Apparently the Russians, for all their supposed political savvy, could not understand the impossibly weak position of the little countries of Eastern Europe and came to think that even a small evidence of democracy was dangerous. Stalin made the well-known remark at Potsdam that "any freely elected government would be anti-Soviet, and that we cannot permit," but was this really an astute observation? There is either a doctrinaire politics here or the operation of an irrational will. Either belies the assertions of the revisionists that an American policy of universalism, in particular the open door in Eastern Europe, was a major reason for the origins of the cold war.

The military advantage of an Eastern European cordon sanitaire proved to be slight. The satellite armies were unreliable, and after Soviet and American acquisition of medium-range and intercontinental ballistic missiles in the 1950s and 1960s the territory of the satellites was of no discernible military value.

The revisionists advanced a third theory about U.S. foreign policy during 1945 and the origins of the cold war: the United States dropped two atomic bombs on the Japanese, not so much to end the war, which was drawing to a finish anyway, but to impress the Russians, who were giving trouble in Eastern Europe. It is pleasant indeed to be able to relate that the brouhaha over Alperovitz's *Atomic Diplomacy: Hiroshima and Potsdam, the Use of the Atomic Bomb and the American Confrontation with Soviet Power,* which began with publication of that sensational volume in 1965, soon was virtually at an end, until, as we will see in Chapter Two, it arose again, in a different form, in 1986. Most of the revisionists so hedged their acceptance of Alperovitz's thesis as almost to remove it from sight, and Alperovitz himself retired from the scene of his triumph, or near disaster, and for a long while turned to other matters. In the preface to a collection of his essays published in 1970 he related that they were his last on foreign policy and that he hoped "to help edit a reader and perhaps help devise some ways to constrain policy, by making it more responsive to popular sentiment.... My future work will be concerned almost exclusively with domestic policy matters and with efforts to transform the political economy of our domestic institutions."[37]

The truth was that, after stimulating much comment with a dramatic thesis and after engaging in several polemical articles in the *New York Review of Books* and so irritating Feis that the latter in his book on the origins of the cold war refused to mention the author of *Atomic Diplomacy* by name, Alperovitz could not prove his major contention. Ulam, in a caustic analysis of "Dr. Alperovitz," wrote,

> One would expect Alperovitz to adduce at least a single instance of an American negotiator saying in effect to a Russian during the period in question (1945–46), "You ought to remember we have the bomb," or "If you go easy on the Poles we might share our nuclear know-how with you." Or he might offer a public statement by an American official that "the Russians ought to keep in mind before they go too far in Romania that we have this weapon." Dr. Alperovitz does not cite any such instances because there weren't any.[38]

His supporters were reduced to saying that Alperovitz widened their horizons, making them see that some officials in the United States believed that the threat of the atomic bomb might help them resolve their troubles with the Russians. Alperovitz was reduced to relying on the powers of psychology: possession of the bomb, he declared, influenced American officials more than they knew or said. In a sideways movement in one of his *New York Review* essays he also took refuge in logic. American military leaders, he remarked, believed the bomb unnecessary for victory over Japan, but the United States failed to reassess the military situation. Why did "the momentum remain when the military reasons disappeared?" Answer: "A diplomatic momentum had by this time taken control of policy."[39]

By the time he had made his retreat, half of the graduate students in the country were believing his original thesis and the other half were looking for holes in his argument. One of the latter at the University of Tennessee found that, when Alperovitz claimed that on June 18, 1945, Truman's military advisers had agreed that Japan could be forced to surrender unconditionally without the use of the bomb and without an invasion (and the diplomatic momentum was, therefore, about to set in) and quoted General Marshall as saying, "the impact of Russian entry on the already hopeless Japanese may well be the decisive action levering them into capitulation," he had trimmed the quotation so as to give it a quite different meaning from what Marshall intended.[40] But just as the Tennessee sharpshooter was about to draw a bead on Alperovitz, the enfant terrible of 1965 was, as mentioned, rapidly disappearing over the historiographical horizon.

3

Revisionist critics of U.S. foreign policy during the cold war era encountered three problems or issues or aspects of policy that came to decision in the year 1946 that bothered them in varying degree. Like the contentions discussed in preceding pages, these also are worth careful notice in what by this juncture may be beginning to appear as an effort to knock down every theory the revisionists put up. Frankly, and at risk of appearing to be a traditionalist, a defender of received truths, and a victim of cold war rhetoric (after all, is there not *some* merit in any position?), I may as well admit that I found it difficult to believe any of their arguments.

The first of the concerns of the revisionists about issues that came to decision in 1946 was a U.S. offer to limit atomic weapons, which to the revisionists appeared not altogether sincere. In view of the developing troubles with the Russians, why would the Americans want to give away the atomic bomb? In the months immediately following Hiroshima and Nagasaki did they not in fact try to use the atomic monopoly to persuade the Russians to be more reasonable? Could not the Baruch Plan of 1946 have been itself a ploy, for instead of making an outright effort to share the atomic secret with the Soviets the United States passed the whole issue to the United Nations and proposed an impossibly hedged program, which only affronted the Russians? These questions, one must say, were germane. The conclusions of Alperovitz, unacceptable in themselves, called attention to the possible use of atomic diplomacy later. Much later, in the 1950s and early 1960s, Khrushchev had been adept at scaring other nations and had some reason to complain of similar ungentlemanly behavior by American leaders. It was understandable that the revisionists would look back into the American atomic past and ask how the United States had behaved during the era when it was Mr. Atomic Bomb. The revisionists were also concerned about what political scientists described as atomic blackmail, which they properly considered indistinguishable from atomic diplomacy (everything depends on who gives and who receives; blackmail is always received).

Now, it is undeniable that Secretary Byrnes, whose actions never amused the revisionists, did talk privately, within the administration, about using the atomic bomb diplomatically. He told Assistant Secretary of War McCloy in August 1945 that he intended to go to the forthcoming London Foreign Ministers Conference with the implied threat of the bomb in his pocket, and Secretary of War Stimson on September 4 recorded in his diary a similar conversation with Byrnes:

I took up the question...how to handle Russia with the big bomb. I found that Byrnes was very much against any attempt to cooperate with

Russia. His mind is full of his problems with the coming meeting of foreign ministers and he looks to having the presence of the bomb in his
pocket, so to speak, as a great weapon to get through the thing.[41]

Stimson was accustomed to dictating into a machine six, eight—even
ten or twelve—doublespaced pages of diary every morning while shav-
ing. The words poured forth without any deliberate thought, so, shortly
after the end of World War II, his detailed diary became a quarry for
investigators of the Pearl Harbor disaster. It became a mine for all sorts
of information about the cold war. While Stimson's diary account of
the Byrnes conversation may be a little stark, it probably is close to the
gist of the conversation.

But what the historian has to add is that, once Byrnes arrived in London for the meeting that began in September and ran into early October 1945, he did not threaten anyone. The closest that researchers can
come to evidence of stern talk at London is some casual conversation
that may not have had any importance. At a cocktail party Molotov,
who according to Foreign Secretary Ernest Bevin was drinking "rather
much, even for him," raised his glass and said, "Here's to the Atom Bomb,"
and added, "We've got it." As is now known, this claim was an exaggeration. Bevin admittedly had become nervous because, during one conference session, Molotov proposed that if Britain would not agree to
allot a former Italian colony in Africa to Russia, the USSR would be
content to have the Belgian Congo. Did that, Bevin wondered, mean
that the Russians wanted uranium?[42] Meanwhile, on the third day of
the conference, Byrnes and Molotov had indulged in some kidding that
took a form that might have had diplomatic overtones but, as most
Americans would admit upon reading what Byrnes said, probably was
just kidding. Molotov in his peculiar way—the Russian possessed a
sardonic sense of humor and liked the droll and sometimes the slightly
macabre—asked Byrnes, rather out of the blue, if the secretary had an
atomic bomb in his side pocket. "You don't know Southerners," was
Byrnes's response. "We carry our artillery in our hip pocket. If you don't
cut out all this stalling and let us get down to work, I am going to pull
an atomic bomb out of my hip pocket and let you have it." Whereupon
Molotov laughed, as did the interpreter. Four nights later, Byrnes was

making a lyrical speech about harmony and cooperation, perhaps a bit on the Irish side, and Molotov paid him a tribute by saying that he really was gifted and, in addition, Byrnes had an atomic bomb.[43]

The revisionists believed that the wartime effort to keep a secret from the Russians was itself almost enough to ensure the postwar breakup of the grand alliance and that only an immediate postwar offer to discuss the problem could have atoned for it. They also contended that the addition of the Baruch Plan, so full of American safeguards that the Russians could not accept it, made the entire chapter of policy impossible to view with any other feeling than that, as the Russians put it, the Americans were scheming to maintain their atomic monopoly.

Still, it is difficult to conclude that the Truman administration did its worst in regard to limitation of atomic weapons. The effort to limit atomic weapons was an unprecedented proposition. The administration had to pay attention to a very sensitive Congress and public. By defying American desires in Eastern Europe the Russians were not exactly helping their own case. When at last the Truman administration, in June 1946, went to the United Nations with the Baruch Plan, it was no effort to dump the issue into the hands of an international body that could do nothing; the UN was clearly not a dispose-all for American negotiators who wanted to keep the bomb. The choice of Baruch as the chief American negotiator may have been unwise, but the time invested in drawing up the Acheson-Lilienthal report, a preliminary report, and then the Baruch Plan was so extensive as to suggest a serious effort on the part of the Americans. If the plan failed, the failure was no proof that the administration wanted it to fail so as to be able to continue to threaten the Soviets with atomic bombs. There was evidence that the president himself had little faith in the bomb as a diplomatic or even military weapon. In the autumn of 1945 when talking with Budget Director Harold D. Smith he commented, according to Smith, "There are some people in the world who do not seem to understand anything except the number of divisions you have." "Mr. President," said Smith, "you have an atomic bomb up your sleeve." "Yes," was the reply, "but I am not sure it can ever be used."[44]

In seeking to find some way of dealing with the Russians, the administration, according to the revisionists, tried economic pressure and botched the job. Could this have been so? One really must raise several doubts, and there is no proof to support the charge. It is possible that, as Schlesinger related, the Russians misinterpreted the abrupt cancellation of lend-lease on May 12, 1945, as blackmail, the American handling of the USSR's request for a large postwar loan as deliberate sabotage, and the ending of reparations from the Western zones of Germany as pro-Germanism. But then, perhaps if the Americans had done everything the Russians wanted on economic issues, nothing would have changed. According to Schlesinger, it "is not clear...that satisfying Moscow on any of these financial scores would have made much essential difference."[45] Moreover, with the exception of one admitted instance of internal administrative confusion, it is hard to see what alternative the Americans had. Such revisionists as Alperovitz, Williams, and Gardner interpreted the sudden cutting off of lend-lease on May 12, 1945, as the use of crude pressure by the Truman administration, but an article by George C. Herring, based on the Stettinius papers at the University of Virginia and unpublished State Department and other records, proved that there was no operant other than administrative failure. The decision to cut off lend-lease was an overly legal decision taken by a few subordinate officials; it applied to all countries and not exclusively to Russia; it was violently opposed by Harriman, Assistant Secretary of State Will Clayton, and Stettinius, and new orders allowed ships at sea to turn around and head for their foreign ports. The Herring article showed how privileged a position Russian lend-lease enjoyed, that the Soviet-American "protocols" or treaties were never the detailed, binding instruments the United States demanded and obtained from the other allies, and that the Soviets anyway were asking, by May, for many items that were not really usable in the war against Japan.[46] The episode bothered American leaders, aware of Russian sensitivity, and Truman's memoirs relate that Stalin at Potsdam was full of talk about the cutting off of lend-lease, although the Potsdam records do not so indicate.

If the American handling of lend-lease in May 1945 was no attempt at economic pressure—and the revisionists afterward admitted as much—there remained the questions of a Russian loan and of American treatment of German reparations. Molotov in January 1945 mentioned a large postwar credit, $6 billion, and said the Soviets would be willing to use the money to buy American goods because such purchases would help to prevent a postwar depression in the United States. Roosevelt asked that nothing be done until he could talk to Stalin. During the Yalta Conference the latter said nothing about a loan, nor did he mention the loan proposal during the talks with Hopkins in Moscow in May 1945, nor during the Potsdam Conference. Why didn't Stalin, so fond of calling attention to the enormous damage the Germans wreaked upon Russia and the unhurt nature of the American economy, then ask the Americans for a loan? Was he too shy?[47]

Not until early 1946 were any steps taken toward negotiating a loan, at which point the proposal of Molotov for $6 billion was cut to $2 billion with conditions put on it that the Russians refused. They wanted a no-strings loan, which made no sense to the Americans. A report within the government estimated that the Soviet economy could recover without American aid, that the Russians could regain their prewar level of capital investment by 1948, and that a loan of $2 billion would speed up reconstruction by only three to four months.[48] It is quite true that during the war the Soviets engaged two-thirds of the German Army, that Russian deaths reached from fifteen to twenty million, compared with perhaps one million for the Western allies, and that the output of Russian industry was halved by the German invasion and transfer of factories to the east. The conclusion is almost inescapable that the Soviets, despite their enormous losses and needs, did not want the loan except under impractically lenient conditions.

As for whether a freely granted loan—what good Protestant Americans sometimes refer to as a freewill offering—might have softened the Soviets' international policies, the revisionist expert on the loan question, Thomas G. Paterson, came to no firmer a conclusion than the following:

> The evidence suggests [sic] that America's refusal to aid Russia through a loan similar to that granted to the British in early 1946, perhaps [sic] contributed [sic] to a continuation of a low standard of living for the Russian people with detrimental international effects [sic], to a less conciliatory and harsher Russian policy toward Germany and Eastern Europe, and to unsettled and inimical postwar Soviet-American relations.[49]

The revisionists cited the failure of the Western allies to live up to the reparations agreements at Yalta and Potsdam as evidence of callousness toward the Russians' wartime suffering and postwar need. Here one must remark that the accords were exceptionally loose, the figure of $20 billion in German reparations—half to go to Russia—being only tentative. When, in subsequent months, the British discovered that their large dollar loan of 1946 was going in fair part to feed, as Chancellor of the Exchequer Hugh Dalton put it, "these bloody Germans," when the Americans discovered that the Germans in the U.S. occupation zone were also on the American taxpayer's back, and when it became evident in 1946 that the joint chiefs of staff paper 1067 would ensure that the Germans and perhaps the rest of the Continent would be on welfare for years, nothing remained but to halt reparations.[50]

In addition to the presentation of the Baruch Plan and the failure of the United States to improve relations with the USSR through economic means, a third concern of the revisionists in reexamining American diplomacy in 1946 was the development, early in the year, of what they liked to describe as cold war rhetoric. Stalin on February 9 spoke of the antagonisms of communism and modern monopoly capitalism; George F. Kennan's eight-thousand-word cable from Moscow arrived in the State Department, analyzing the historic and ideological and psychological roots of Russian intransigence; Churchill in March spoke at Fulton, Missouri, and Stalin riposted with a newspaper interview comparing Churchill and Hitler. Also in March, the United States expelled the Russians from northern Iran, in which locality the Russians were trying to get an oil concession and were encouraging Azerbaijani separatism.

The oratorical aspect of the first weeks of 1946 is undeniable. Although largely a Russian-British argument, with the Soviets attacking America's British ally in the person of its former leader, the contentions on both sides were surely intended for their effect on the United States. The oil aspect of the Iranian crisis was difficult to measure, may not have been serious, and in any event was secondary. Russian encouragement of separatism followed a pattern in Eastern Europe, where the Red Army dominated politics in the areas it occupied. The Soviets certainly overstayed their leave in Iran; by agreement with the Americans and the British they had committed themselves to depart by March 2, 1946. What prompted them to get out was unclear. That the Americans were giving in to Churchill's anticommunism seemed doubtful and has not been proved. Adam Ulam advanced the piquant theory that the Russians scampered out of Iran because Churchill had just accused them of imperialism and they did not want to provide an obvious proof.[51] There is some indication that the Iranian premier of the moment was a wily old operator who held a diplomatic card or two under the table for dickering with the Soviets when his American partner was not looking. Truman, in a press conference in 1952, told of a presidential ultimatum to the Russians and repeated this account in his memoirs as well as in a book entitled *Truman Speaks,* published in 1960, and in a conversation with Herbert Druks in 1962. A volume of *Foreign Relations* contained an editorial note to the effect that records in the State Department and in the Department of Defense contained absolutely no indication of an ultimatum and that several former high officers of the State Department who were queried about this issue had no memory of one.[52] The department's records later opened to researchers, who could check the department's veracity on this interesting point and perhaps uncover some real skulduggery in the Iranian crisis—maybe some Anglo-American cooperation concerning the Churchillian half of "the appropriate declarations of cold war," as LaFeber called the exchanges between Churchill and Stalin.[53]

4

In 1947, which Theodore H. White in *Fire in the Ashes* termed "the Year of Divergence," U.S. foreign policy took an avowed turn against Soviet foreign policy that could either be accounted the beginning of the cold war or, as the *New York Times* put the situation in terms of U.S. foreign relations since 1775, the end of an epoch of isolation and occasional intervention and the beginning of an epoch of American responsibility.[54] So historic a situation did not escape the cold war revisionists, and they labored mightily to show how the Truman Doctrine, the Marshall Plan, and the decision to give the Germans in the U.S.-British zones independence were not the great, signal chapters marking the beginning of a new epoch of American responsibility but merely more evidence of the Truman administration's depravity and stupidity. No anticommunistic horn of Roland sounded forth from revisionist books to echo through the valleys and across the mountains of civilization. None of that nonsense for them. Readers of their books and articles had no feeling at all for the alarm, the confusion, the sinking hopes of individuals, leaders and publics alike, in Washington and in Western Europe, when the rigorous winter of 1946–1947 brought Europe's economies almost to a standstill and when the early springtime gave every evidence of what the military analyst for the *New York Times,* Hanson W. Baldwin (who to the revisionists was a repellant old hawk), reported as a crisis akin to the fall of the Roman Empire. The revisionists heard only a few tumbles backstage as they quietly analyzed the scene in Washington and Western Europe that spring of 1947, and though they conceded some nobility to the Marshall Plan, they on balance found American policy of that time to have been no great, successful rescue operation but a deplorable, uncalled-for movement into cold war confrontation.

The Truman Doctrine, they said, was first of all unnecessary because the administration misread the situation in Greece. The truth was, they averred (and in this single observation they were probably correct), that the Greek guerrillas were not receiving help from Stalin, that the dictator later told the Yugoslav communist Milovan Djilas that the guerrillas were not getting support, that instead they were receiving it from Marshal Tito's Yugoslavia. Only a year or so after the American intervention in the Greek civil war, Tito for his own good reason—his split with the Russians—closed his country's border with Greece and began to force an end to the civil war, after which the Greek Stalinists gained control of the guerrillas, went over from guerrilla actions to set-piece battles with the revived Greek Army, and lost, giving up the fight in October 1949. The revisionists, leaning heavily on a thirty-five-page account by Barnet, related that at no time during the American decision to create the Truman Doctrine did the Department of State try to analyze the guerrilla situation in Greece to determine if intervention was really necessary.[55]

To take the latter point first, until 1972 the revisionists did not have much knowledge of what the Department of State knew in 1947 because the American documents had not yet been published in *Foreign Relations*. Offhand, it did seem unlikely that so large and smart an outfit as the State Department would have failed to do its homework on the guerrilla problem, although the department could not have known about Stalin's conversation with Djilas, which took place in 1948 and was not published until 1962. The fifth volume of the *Foreign Relations* series for 1947 appeared in 1972 and contained 484 pages on the Greek-Turkish situation. It did not include any detailed department analysis of the Greek guerrilla problem prior to announcement of the Truman Doctrine. But this was no proof that the department had failed to make such an analysis, for the documents in *Foreign Relations* were only a selection. The department's archives for 1947 were not opened to researchers until mid-1973.

As for the allegiance of the Greek communists, there seemed little reason to dispute Barnet's analysis—except its conclusions. After all, was the factionalism of the Greek communists—their willingness to defy Stalin and accept aid from Tito—important? Three arguments say it was not. First, no one in 1947 anticipated Tito's expulsion from the Cominform in 1948; whatever Stalin's desires in regard to the guerrillas' behavior, the Department of State had to proceed on the assumption that, if Stalin could not get to the guerrillas, then he could get to Tito, who could do the job. Second, it is an interesting and pertinent fact that after Tito's expulsion the Greek communists split on tactics and the Stalinist faction got control—which says that the faction on top in earlier years might not have stayed on top. The third point is that, if it had not been for the outbreak of the Korean War, Stalin might have wiped out Tito, in which case where would have been the Titoist, national Greek communists? The whole business of the Greek guerrillas, and to whom (Greece, Tito, or Stalin) they momentarily owed allegiance, strikes one as too volatile a situation for any prudent statesman at the time to have relied on.

The revisionists aptly pointed out, maybe with some exaggeration, the undemocratic nature of the regime in Athens, a fact that was well known in Washington in 1947. They enjoyed showing how the regime in Ankara also did not exactly represent the apotheosis of democracy, likewise a commonplace of the time. The Turkish foreign situation differed from that in Greece in that the Russians were not employing guerrillas but putting direct diplomatic pressure on Turkey to get concessions along the straits and on the Turkish-Soviet border, forcing the Turks to maintain an army that the impoverished country could not afford. There was indeed a threat to Turkey, but the United States in 1945 and 1946 had said little about it publicly. As in many other conflicts with the Soviets, the United States hoped this one could be quietly resolved.

Some people at the time thought that the administration had gratuitously included Turkey in the Truman Doctrine. Gardner, who had an unerring eye for a good quotation, noted the remark of a witness at one of the congressional hearings in 1947 that when "the new dish was being prepared for American consumption, Turkey was slipped into the oven with Greece because that seemed to be the surest way to cook a tough bird." The revisionists also repeated with approval the judgment of Byrnes's *Speaking Frankly:* "We did not have to decide that the Turkish Government and the Greek monarchy were outstanding examples of free and democratic governments."[56]

But what bothered the cold war critics more than anything else about the Truman Doctrine was that they saw it as an appalling piece of cold war rhetoric. They believed that the doctrine gave an enormous push to the anticommunism of American public opinion and that it eventually turned upon its authors when Senator Joseph R. McCarthy accused the Truman administration of being itself soft on communism; they believed also that the rhetoric (they were fond of the word) lasted into the 1950s with bad results, for the secretary of state for most of that decade believed in anticommunism as fervently as he did in Presbyterianism; and then in the 1960s the rhetoric took us into Vietnam.

This was a remarkable accusation, and it was ventilated not merely in the random assertions of revisionist books and articles but in two volumes devoted to the point. One of them, by Richard M. Freeland, suggested to its *New York Times* reviewer, Christopher Lehmann-Haupt, the simile of an airplane ride, whereby foreign policy looks different from the air (where Freeland was, with his documents, quotations, and theories) than from the ground (where Lehmann-Haupt himself could view it with his recollections of the occasions and purposes of 1947).[57] It should be impossible to believe that Harry S. Truman was the inventor or, if not that, the chief distributor of anticommunism. It is true, however, that anyone can believe anything he wants, like the White Queen in *Through the Looking Glass,* who made it her business to believe six impossible things every morning before breakfast. Ronald Steel believed that Acheson was the real villain in the anticommunization of his fellow citizens: Acheson knew what might happen, but to get the administration's measures through Congress and to win the approbation of the public he willingly gave the American people strong injections of anticommunism.[58]

The allegation was so large that it was difficult to put down. Suffice it to say that it showed more faith in the efficacy of a single speech—Truman's address to Congress, in which Acheson had a large hand—than one ordinarily would expect. Moreover, if Acheson, as Steel said, showed a contempt for the American people by subjecting them to all those anticommunism shots, could one not turn this commentary around and say that the revisionists themselves showed a contempt for the American people, to think that the public was so gullible that a little campaign from official Washington could manipulate their minds? Arthur Vandenberg is alleged to have said to Truman, a few days before the president delivered the Truman Doctrine address of March 12, that it was necessary to scare hell out of the country. Memories of the Vandenberg remark differ, and he may not have said just that. The address was not all that scary, though the administration sought to put the Greek-Turkish issue into the large framework it deserved. Years later, George Kennan remarked his personal sadness that the Truman Doctrine had become a worldwide program—though it is not clear that it ever did, even under John Foster Dulles, not to mention the administrations of Lyndon B. Johnson and Richard M. Nixon. It is certain that the Truman administration had no such intention before the speech, nor did it behave that way afterward. If in subsequent months and years there was a lot of talk about anticommunism, the talk had something to do with such non-Truman-connected occurrences as the collapse of China, the invasion of South Korea, Whittaker Chambers's production of the pumpkin papers, the confession of Klaus Fuchs, or Senator McCarthy's rare gifts for invention and invective. As another *New York Times* reviewer, William V. Shannon, put it, "Truman was more often the victim than the progenitor of that time of troubles."[59]

As the revisionists nitpicked the Truman Doctrine, they similarly attempted to do a job on the Marshall Plan. They said that it divided Europe, as Marshall expected it to do, and that even in its largesse it was an American policy instead of an international policy. Once more they failed to show the enormous need for a program, the hectic pressure of events, and the unattractive prospect of aiding Russia when the Soviets were opposing American policy in Europe, and they did not stress the program's economic success. The cold war critics averred that the invitation Marshall extended to the Soviets to join in the plan was meant to be a ploy. Charles E. Bohlen, they said, confessed that both he and Kennan gave Marshall this advice. It does not follow that "the Marshall Plan was," as Paterson suggested, "a weapon against Russia rather than a magnanimous, no-strings-attached undertaking to relieve destitute Europeans."[60] As for Paterson's objection to unilateral American action and his suggestion that the Marshall Plan could have been handled by an international organization unconnected with cold war rhetoric, such as the Economic Commission for Europe, it carried a surface plausibility later when so many individuals had so little comprehension of the problems of 1947. There were some who recalled the weakness of international organizations, the need to prevent the turning of U.S. funds against their donor, the need to prevent funds being poured down the drain (with or without Russian connivance), the unwillingness of Congress and the public to give money without strings, the fact that no banker in his right mind would lend (it was of course a gift, but the analogy holds) money on a house—attempting to aid Russian recovery—he had not seen and without a financial statement.[61]

A third allegation against the Truman administration's policies in 1947 deserves little discussion in detail. This is the charge that they helped bring on the cold war by dividing Germany, which thereby created the postwar result the Russians most feared—a rich, strong, rearmed, if somewhat fragmented German nation. The result was beyond question, but no good historian should work back from the result to the cause unless he wants to go all the way—which the revisionists did not, for that would mess up their usable past. The prime responsibility for the state of affairs in Germany, as Klaus Epstein wrote, rested with the late Adolf Hitler.[62] An award for the Division of Germany, Second Class, must go to the Russians, who in their German policy faced a serious problem at the end of World War II: the Germans—because of a long heritage of anti-Russian feeling, anticommunism, the appalling behavior of the occupying Red Army, the expulsion of twelve million East Germans, and impossible reparations—hated the Russians. It was clear that in any fair election East Germany would have voted to unite with the West. Russian offers to unify Germany, as Epstein contended, could have been nothing other than propaganda, for the Soviets would not have gained control of the other zones and would have lost their own. But over the years the Russians produced a mighty propaganda about their desire to unify Germany, and many people began to believe it, and in this manner the West divided Germany. Gradually, on the American side, the economic and military reasons for unifying the western zones began to become apparent. Bizonia was created on January 1, 1947, and everything followed therefrom, albeit with skillful Russian assistance (the murder of Jan Masaryk, the Czechoslovakian foreign minister and son of the nation's first president, ensured passage of the Marshall Plan, and the plan included participation by West Germany; the Berlin blockade ensured the carrying out of the London Recommendations of June 1948 for a West German government; the Korean War galvanized the United States into incorporating West Germany into NATO).

On two occasions, early in 1947 and then much later, in 1952, the Soviets gave signs of willingness to unify Germany. In 1952 they said they would allow "elections" in East Germany so long as there was neutralization. The West turned down these opportunities because, as Acheson described the offer of 1952, the timing was so suspicious that it looked like a golden apple of discord tossed over the iron curtain. The revisionists thought the United States should have taken a bite out of those apples, and their opponents agreed with Acheson.

Gardner, looking for earlier evidence of American stupidity in Germany, claimed that the creation of Bizonia occurred in part because

General Lucius D. Clay was worried stiff about socialism. Gimbel said this theory was a figment of imagination.[63]

In summary, what can be said about President Truman and the revisionists? The controversy rose and fell in just a few years when the mostly young historical scholars of that persuasion wrote their books and articles and then, suddenly, ceased writing and turned to other things. It seems clear that the end of the Vietnam War, which was foreseen in 1972 when the United States withdrew its troops, and occurred in 1975 when the North Vietnam Army overwhelmed the American-supported regime in Saigon, was the reason the scholarship stopped, or so one cannot help but suspect. Through all the accusations about the American president of 1945–1953 and the course of American foreign policy there was the undercurrent of Vietnam, and it was more than that, for the Vietnam War gave support to the idea that American policy had turned into a dangerous course in 1945 and was passing out of control, the Truman Doctrine expanding to the entire world, Americans willing to fight any fight, anywhere. Whatever, the demise of revisionism as an active field of scholarship coincided, interestingly, with the end of intervention in Vietnam.

But there was a residue, an aftermath, that has been troublesome to individuals like myself who have sought to carry out, in our historical writings, the tradition of the great historian Leopold von Ranke, the task of trying to capture the past as it really was, *wie es eigentlich gewesen ist*. Actually most of us did not believe entirely in Ranke; we knew that it was impossible to bring back what in every detail had happened. We knew that historical writing necessarily was imperfect, what had passed into memory from aids to memory, known as documents, could never be captured in entirety. There always would be gaps, uncertainties. Many events of the past could not be recovered. Our task was to do what we could with what lay at hand. What troubled us was that our young revisionist friends believed that whatever they could put together, leaving out what was inconvenient, was the procedure in writing about the past—that if they had an idea in mind, a theory about the past, they could assemble its supports and proceed from there, the wish being father to the thought. If Vietnam was proof of a tendency toward disaster in American foreign policy, their task was to gather the supports and make the point. Historians from time immemorial had done that sort of thing, they believed; everyone started with a thesis and advanced to its proofs. Nothing wrong with that.

This violation of the canons of scholarship that constituted the center of the revisionist technique has had a marked effect on historical scholarship, no doubt; it has continued, very much visible, in scholarly analyses of the position of the United States in the world down to the present writing. So much of what appears as historical truth is naught but an effort to bend or turn policy toward what writers deem proper.

Two

The Bomb—the View from Washington

In long retrospect, now more than fifty years, it is safe to say that not merely has cold war revisionism in general—over a bewildering variety of claims about the presidential administration of Harry S. Truman—come to an unlamented end, but the single remaining contention of some present-day historians, political scientists, and publicists, over the use of nuclear weapons against wartime Japan, has run its course. Briefly, questioning of the bombings of August 6 and 9, 1945, had its scholarly beginnings in the United States with publication in 1965 of the book by Alperovitz entitled *Atomic Diplomacy.* Alperovitz claimed that the United States dropped the bombs on Japan to impress and intimidate the Russians. The argument had a certain attraction, for it explained the cold war. It fell to earth because of sheer lack of proof that any American statesman confronted a Russian with such a scheme. Nuclear revisionism flared again when in 1986 the historian Barton Bernstein of Stanford University advanced a new contention, that an invasion of Japan, had it occurred, would have cost far fewer casualties than President Truman claimed in his memoirs.[1] According to this argument the postwar statements by Truman and by former secretary of war Stimson, that an invasion might have cost half a million or a million American dead, or at the least that many casualties (with dead running on a scale of one to three or one to four), were made only to justify an ill-thought-out decision to use nuclear weapons. Not long afterward several scholars entered the lists. First in the field was Edward J. Drea with his remarkable *MacArthur's ULTRA: Codebreakers and the War against Japan, 1942–1945,* published in 1992. When the fiftieth anniversary of the bombings approached in 1995, and it was clear that the Bernstein thesis was going to receive support in several books, opponents were ready for the onslaught. Their books—I speak of those by Robert J. Maddox, Thomas B. Allen and Norman Polmar, and Robert P. Newman—nearly finished off nuclear revisionism. D. M. Giangreco has weighed in against Bernstein on the numbers issue, with telling results. The coup de grace was given by the Japanese historian Sadao Asada, in a notable article in the *Pacific Historical Review.*[2]

My task in the obsequies for nuclear revisionism is to relate the view from Washington.[3] I wish to say that it was impossible for such a hard-working, intelligent president as Truman not to have learned that the numbers issue—the Japanese buildup on the southernmost home island, Kyushu—was very serious, justifying use of nuclear weapons upon Japanese cities.[4] I say also that it would not have been possible for the president's principal military adviser—the army's chief of staff, General Marshall—to have misled Truman by withholding information from him on this point.

The appearance of Truman in the presidency marked a radical change in the view from Washington, a remarkable change from the languid incompetence of the last year, perhaps much of the third presidential term, of Franklin Roosevelt. In Roosevelt's last year as president his physical condition was such that he may have spent no more than an hour a day on his official duties.[5] The president was in heart failure and physically could not see many people, nor for long. Only two years in age separated Roosevelt and Truman, the difference between being born in 1882 and in 1884. Physically there was an enormous difference. In his last year FDR did not possess the stamina to handle the responsibilities of his high office. He barely could keep up appearances. It is doubtful if detailed, complicated papers obtained serious readings. With Truman's entry into the presidency all this slowness, or these lapses, came to a sudden end. Truman often was at his desk at 6:00 a.m., an unheard-of hour for Roosevelt.

Truman was not only able to handle much more of the business of the White House than had Roosevelt: over the many years Truman had proved himself a reader in ways that Roosevelt never did. FDR accumulated a large personal library and made a practice of signing his name in his books; the Hyde Park books were impressive in their numbers and range. But a story went around Washington during Roosevelt's presidency that FDR never read a book. His close friend and second postmaster general, Frank C. Walker, was inclined to believe it. In his recently published autobiography he remarked on the test, so to speak, that a Roosevelt visitor gave the president. The visitor asked the president if he had read the naughty novel of 1944 by Kathleen Winsor, *Forever Amber.* Roosevelt replied with a grin, "Only the dirty parts."[6] Truman's attachment to the written word, his willingness to read rather than listen to someone, an arrangement I might add that is five times as effective as talk, was legendary.[7] Not all the stories, including some of his own, were true. In high school he did not read all the books in the Independence public library, including the encyclopedias, as he claimed. During his eleven years on the farm, 1906–1917, he had little time. He began to read again, in the literature of American history, mostly biographies of his heroes such as Jefferson and Jackson, only in the last years of his life when confined to his Independence house. But during the long years of public service he also was well known for going through the documents that crossed his desk, skimming if necessary, otherwise reading them in detail. In the Roosevelt Library at Hyde Park there are few evidences of FDR's documentary reading. In the Truman Library are massive annotations of state papers, often humorous remarks by a president who was carefully reviewing the material crossing his desk.

Truman received criticism for making snap decisions, and that point assuredly adverse to his reputation needs examination, for it was nothing more than a myth. Richard E. Neustadt, who was a member of the

Truman administration, wrote that when Truman saw a problem he at once wanted to make a decision. This contention, alas, had no foundation in fact. After Truman left the presidency he sometimes occupied himself with writing short essays, perhaps for eventual presentation at the Truman Library, a place he envisioned as a regional, multistate center for study of the presidency. In one of these essays he admitted that when he saw a problem he made a decision. He described it as a "jump decision," a tentative conclusion. After which, he wrote, he would think about it, mull it over, speak with his advisers and with whoever else knew something about it. He thought of it during his morning walks, and during early mornings at his desk, before the assistants came in. Then, and only at the last possible moment, beyond which a decision would be too late, would he reach a conclusion—after which he refused to reconsider, for, to use the old metaphor, the die had been cast.

One could contend that within the government in Washington, because he was new to the presidency and also because the war was coming to an end (it ended in Europe on May 8, 1945), Truman received little or no advice. It is true that the changeover from the Roosevelt to the Truman administration was not easy. When Truman became president he found little loyalty among members of the White House and executive office staffs, or within the cabinet, and had to bring in people from his vice presidential office, from among his Senate friends, and from his home state of Missouri. He said privately that staffing was no easy task, he did not know enough "big" people, and that while he had a wide acquaintance in Missouri the politicians he knew there were often small, courthouse types. But in considering such huge issues as the use of nuclear weapons on Japanese cities there is no evidence that Truman's initial staffing problems, and there were a few, had any bearing at all.

As one might have expected of a president with the aforementioned qualities, Truman took the measure of his responsibilities in deciding upon the use of nuclear weapons. The process was as logical as it could be. At the outset, one must add, the bomb was not considered an issue, for the bomb's power was a large question mark. At the time of a June 18, 1945, meeting in the White House with the service secretaries, the joint chiefs of staff, and the undersecretary of state, to make a final decision on the invasion of Japan, there had been no test of the bomb that the scientists were building from uranium, nor could there be, for the amount of uranium extracted from the gaseous diffusion plant at Oak Ridge, Tennessee, was so small that there was only enough "bomb stuff" for a single explosion—that is, its use as a weapon. Production of plutonium from the centrifuges at Hanford, Washington, was another matter, with the prospect of a series of weapons of increasing yield, the second due in late August; the first plutonium bomb required a test to see if it would work. The uranium bomb was likely to work, but no one knew its TNT equivalent, nor would they know until years after its explosion at Hiroshima, when scientists determined its TNT equivalent at thirteen kilotons, this by measurement of the surviving buildings. Word on the TNT equivalent of the plutonium bomb was uncertain until its test at Alamogordo, New Mexico, which occurred on July 16, nearly a month after the White House meeting on the invasion of Japan. Scientists at the plutonium test varied widely in their estimates, most of them within a range of five hundred to fifteen hundred tons of TNT. They placed their bets in a pool. Two latecomers chose the extremes, zero and twenty thousand, the latter winning when the plutonium device came in at nineteen thousand—but again this wisdom was denied the participants at the June 18 meeting. Meanwhile they knew another limiting factor in the effectiveness of bombs, that a doubling of any TNT equivalent did not double the destruction, which increased by a factor of the cube root, rather than the square root.

The issue of casualties lay at the center of the June 18 discussions. And here Giangreco has discovered new information, namely that the reason for the meeting was a memorandum sent personally to Truman by former president Herbert Hoover. The predecessor of Roosevelt suggested that an invasion could cost half a million American lives. Truman seized upon this memo and sent memoranda asking for a written judgment from each recipient: to Secretary of State Stettinius, who was at the San Francisco Conference; Undersecretary of State Joseph C. Grew; the service secretaries, Forrestal and Stimson; the director of the Office of War Mobilization and Reconversion, Fred M. Vinson; and former secretary of state Cordell Hull.[8]

How does Giangreco's discovery affect the casualties argument? First of all, it must be said, it is a challenge to the Bernstein contention that there is no high-level document for either the Roosevelt or the Truman administration (the latter between the dates of April 12 and August 6, 1945) that displays the prospect of half a million or more deaths or casualties. Moreover, Bernstein has argued that the many versions of JCS 924, the plan of the joint chiefs of staff for the invasion of Japan, did not carry the contention of the JCS 924/2 that an invasion would cost half a million deaths and "many times that number wounded" (this was the ratio of deaths to wounded necessary to kill seven Japanese soldiers on Saipan). The original version of JCS 924 appeared in mid-1944, 924/2 came out on August 30 of that year, 924/16 appeared in April 1945. Bernstein did not understand that each version, unless specifically remarked, continued to carry the text of preceding versions. In addition the Giangreco discovery not only shows that Truman knew about such a high figure in advance of the June 18 meeting, having received it from Hoover, but makes possible the assertion that former president Hoover had come across the number through his manifold high-level contacts within the American government. The editor of the *Army and Navy Journal,* Cal O'Laughlin, was in touch with the former president, and the two men may well have discussed the half million figure; the O'Laughlin letters in the Hoover Library at West Branch, Iowa, are voluminous. O'Laughlin had high-level contacts in Washington and could easily have heard about JCS 924. It is true that possible high-casualty figures were appearing in newspapers, planted by Admiral Chester W. Nimitz's press organization. But one must assume that Hoover would not have written Truman about a figure taken from a newspaper, and that it came from JCS 924.[9]

Truman was exercised about the half million figure, no question about that. His often quoted remark during the June 18 meeting was that he did not want to have another Okinawa "from one end of Japan to the other." With this as background it also should be clear that General Marshall's mention at the meeting of the figure for the first month of the invasion of Luzon, 31,000 casualties, was not a one-for-one statement of casualties anticipated on Kyushu but the introduction of a ratio—31,000 casualties necessary to defeat Japanese forces on Luzon represented one American casualty for every five Japanese casualties—after which one would apply the ratio to the much larger situation on Kyushu. The same went for the figure of 63,000 casualties on Okinawa, which Admiral Leahy put in his diary and introduced at the June 18 meeting only as a percentage of U.S. troop strength on Okinawa. The two figures of 31,000 and 63,000 were benchmarks for ratios, not absolute figures for prospective losses on Kyushu. This said nothing about losses in the subsequent invasion of Honshu, the so-called Tokyo plain, scheduled for March 1, 1946.

It has been said, and this might appear to offer an opening to revisionists, that during the meeting General Marshall avoided serious numbers because he did not wish to turn the president against the forthcoming invasion. The supposition does an injustice to Marshall, who was never known to have been a schemer. Years earlier, when former secretary of war Harry Woodring was angry with everyone in the Roosevelt administration, having himself entered a political doghouse, he wrote privately that Marshall would have sold his own grandmother, but this conclusion never was drawn by anyone other than Woodring, whose name today is not a household word.

And so by the time of the meeting of June 18 the president knew of the casualty figure mentioned in JCS 924. He must have seen other evidence of the anticipated ferocity of defense on the Japanese home islands. Draft calls were increasing; large military call-ups had come to his attention, for they were politically sensitive. He might well have discovered that the army was ordering half a million Purple Heart medals, and army medics were anticipating heavy use of hospital ships and base hospitals.[10] He would have put together all the evidence. He would have had to have been quite a different person to ignore this information.

During the Potsdam Conference, just prior to the bombings, the president had easy access to Marshall, who was at the scene. At the beginning of the conference Stimson was present. It is unbelievable that Marshall and Stimson would not have told Truman of the rapid Japanese buildup on Kyushu.

But by then the plutonium test device had proved equal to nineteen thousand tons of TNT, and more than balanced the increasing danger of an invasion.

THREE

Diplomacy without Armaments

"Diplomacy without armaments," Frederick the Great once said, "is like music without instruments." The thought bears repetition when one looks back over American diplomacy in the twentieth century, and especially when one thinks of the early postwar years, the half decade from the end of the Pacific War in 1945 until the beginning of the Korean War in 1950. Here was a dangerous time in world affairs, if ever such might have been discerned in all the half decades, decades, and even centuries since the rise of nation-states at the beginning of the modern era. Here was a time when American officials, finding themselves in trouble with the Soviet Union, did not have the military wherewithal to back up what they said and sometimes did. We must remind ourselves that during the years when the United States tried to arrive at a modus vivendi with the Soviet Union, and passed through successive crises attempting the task, the forces and armaments with which the country confronted the USSR were far from adequate.

In setting out what the United States did against its Soviet opponents, observers and later historians have tended to write as if America's good intentions should have persuaded the country's antagonists in Moscow. Seldom does one read that the military forces with which the American side sought to oppose the Soviets were not at all impressive, that the Americans were dealing from a terribly weak hand, that both in conventional and nuclear power the American side was incapable, if its full dimensions had been known, of impressing Stalin. Had there been a full disclosure of the nation's military power, we might now assume, many of the conversations and meetings in faraway places and debates in the United Nations organization and elsewhere, the pourparlers that sometimes failed but sometimes succeeded, would have failed promptly and irrevocably.

1

The conventional military strength of the United States in 1945–1950 was deplorable. The favorite general of American GIs, Omar N. Bradley, appears to have told the collaborator on his autobiography, published posthumously, that in the immediate postwar years the U.S. Army could not have fought its way out of a paper bag.[1] The root administrative cause of this predicament was the point system with which the army, and to some extent the navy, began demobilization. The system has almost been forgotten, although it was well known to soldiers and sailors of the time. The idea was to allow for an orderly demobilization and at the same time permit real veterans, compared with soldiers who had only completed a few weeks or months of service, to get out first. After World War I, demobilization had been chaotic, leading to much ill will, principally because the navy in 1918–1919 did not have enough ships to bring the two million troops home immediately from France. This was not the problem after World War II, although there were delays in the Pacific because of the enormous distances. The point system in itself, with some exceptions, was not the problem, for the system gave points for being in the army or navy, for serving abroad, and for serving in combat zones, though it also gave points for possessing a wife and children, which, to single veterans, seemed unfair. The trouble with the point system was that as veterans passed into the depots and to ships for the voyage home, a game of musical chairs developed within units that remained abroad or, for that matter, within units at home that included veterans. As each slot in a unit opened, it had to be filled, and each filler in turn required a substitute at the post from which he came. There was chaos within companies, battalions, regiments, divisions, and all support organizations. The point system became the best possible device for ruining the efficiency of the U.S. Army and Navy.

A much less important reason for organizational chaos after the war was the decision by planners in 1945 to try to hold on to experienced men and women, if necessary by maintaining wartime ranks. The services soon found themselves with an enormous number of high-ranked individuals, enlisted and officer—especially officer. To measure the result in terms of inefficiency would require a sociologist, or a team of them, but suffice it to say that the surfeit of ranks turned in on itself. Matters reached the point where there was a general for every thousand enlisted ranks.

The army decided—and the decision was understandable at first in terms of the need to keep an infrastructure for mobilization—to hold most of the "forts" and posts and cantonments maintained during the war. It thus required an immense force simply to garrison its possessions in the United States and abroad.

As if these obstructions to a lithe, smooth military organization were not enough, there was the decision, which was inevitable, to create a third military service. Such was done de facto during the war through the practical independence of the U.S. Army Air Forces. But in 1947 the air force achieved formal independence, with all the duplication that entailed, including new blue uniforms. The institutionalizing of this change, which of course required an air force academy, absorbed the energies of ranking officers who might have concentrated on organizing their new service in an efficient way.

The enlisted members of the postwar army, navy, and air force were mostly volunteers. The services wanted to try to attract men, rather than force them, and the humors of the many former conscripts were such that they celebrated this arrangement. The inefficiencies of voluntarism need hardly be addressed. There were too few volunteers for the army, and it was necessary to go over to a draft. Meanwhile, the public relations people took money from the services to advertise their attractiveness, an enterprise that may not have increased national preparedness. It is true that after 1945 many veterans stayed in the reserves and were available in case of need; for a while there was this foundation under voluntarism. But it was an uneasy situation, and the foundation eroded as the years passed.

During 1945–1950 the successor to Roosevelt did his best to hold down budget requests for the services, which gave rise to problems without number. Let it be added that Truman had excellent reason to hold down the budgets. He was greatly concerned that the national budget be balanced and, if possible, wanted surpluses to retire the wartime debt, which was ten times the dollar amount of the debt after World War I. Despite all the talk that Truman was another loose-spending Democrat, garnished by stories of how he was naught but a failed haberdasher, he was a fiscal conservative. Surprisingly, too, during the eight national budgets of his time, four were in deficit, four in surplus.

The president's control of the budget gave rise to rebellions within the defense establishment, which subtracted from readiness. Now forgotten, the rebellions were serious. The shoehorning necessary to create the air force and bring the three services together in what was at first described as an establishment, later as the Department of Defense, required negotiations of months, even years. Then the air force immediately wanted more money, and the navy, fearful for retirement of its wartime fleet, which was larger than all the navies of the world put together, soon was fighting for what it considered its life. Indeed, the entire postwar half decade was marked by ferocious interservice rivalries that drained many energies.

The result was a conventional force of dubious credibility for support of the Truman administration vis-à-vis the Soviet Union. Testimony to that fact appeared early in the administration, a question of what to do concerning the Palestine problem, the proposed division of the British mandate into Arab and Jewish portions. There was concern among the Americans and the British that the Soviets might intervene. Perhaps it was the Truman Doctrine that kept them out, or maybe the 1946 UN controversy concerning Soviet failure to leave Iran. Whatever, the Soviets kept out of the Palestine question. The Americans, however, to the chagrin of the British, were involved because of pressure on the Democratic administration by the Jewish lobby, whose strength centered in New York City. Secretary of Defense James V. Forrestal, concerned about Arab displeasure and the threat to the navy's oil supplies in Saudi Arabia, liked to talk in cabinet meetings and elsewhere of how the hapless British could not keep peace in Palestine with sixty thousand troops and that it would require twice that number of UN troops, presumably American, to enforce any UN resolution. The U.S. Army could not provide that many troops. Fortunately the whole issue was determined, largely in the way the administration desired, by the preponderance of force exercised by the Jews in Palestine. But it was an embarrassment not to be able to underwrite UN arrangements in a postage stamp–size area.

A more serious situation arose in relation to the Berlin blockade of 1948–1949, produced by Soviet antipathy toward the London recommendations of June 1948 allowing an essentially independent West German government in Bonn. General Lucius D. Clay, the military governor of the U.S. zone, together with Ambassador Robert D. Murphy, favored sending an armed convoy by rail to Berlin. Truman's other advisers did not want that, for, in case of a shoot-out or even a stalemate (if, say, the Soviets routed the convoy to a siding, letting it sit there without supplies of any sort), the force would have to fight or retreat. The troops available within West Germany, in the American and British zones, were not good enough to oppose the Red Army. A fortuitous event, the institution of an airlift, freed the administration from having to withdraw from Berlin, given that the U.S. Army was incapable of defending the American position.

Throughout negotiation of the Treaty of Dunkirk between Great Britain and France, then the Brussels Pact with the addition of the Benelux countries (Belgium, the Netherlands, and Luxembourg), and finally the North Atlantic Treaty of 1949, the unspoken fact was that Western troops were incapable of resisting the Soviet Army. Strategic plans, as they were called, all were plans for withdrawal, words carefully chosen as to how troops would move backward, some to Channel ports, others to Spain and Portugal. The very idea of holding any line at all was confined to the Rhine, hardly a position from which to defend West Germany, and even that was a tentative proposition, with explanations of what would happen when that line collapsed. The British and continental nations in NATO did not have equipment and could not afford any. The French, unsure they wished to send a military contingent, looked sideways to imperial responsibilities in Algeria and Indochina. There never was any serious force available to NATO until after the start of the Korean War, when in 1951 the United States sent four divisions to reinforce the two there, and especially when a few years later West Germany entered NATO and promised to furnish twelve divisions. Before the Korean War changed worldwide equations, Western forces opposing the Russians in Europe were hardly worthy of the name. It was a remark of that era, 1945–1950, that if Soviet troops desired to conquer Western Europe, all they needed were shoes.

Testimony to the lack of conventional forces came years later in the Bradley autobiography, in which Bradley or his collaborator not only referred to U.S. forces not being able to fight their way out of a paper bag but also remarked that half of the 552,000 officers and men of the army "were overseas on occupation duty, serving as policemen or clerks. The other half were in the States performing various administrative chores."[2] General Marshall, back in the Pentagon in 1950 as secretary of defense, told a small audience that he had been helpless in 1947–1949 when he was secretary of state.

> I remember, when I was Secretary of State, I was being pressed constantly, particularly when in Moscow [the Moscow Conference of Foreign Ministers, 1947], by radio message after radio message to give the Russians hell. . . . When I got back I was getting the same appeal in relation to the Far East and China. At that time, my facilities for giving them hell—and I am a soldier and know something about the ability to give hell—was 1 1/3 divisions over the entire United States. This is quite a proposition when you deal with somebody with over 260 and you have 1 1/3. We had nothing in Alaska. We did not have enough to defend the air strip at Fairbanks.[3]

2

But was not the United States protected by nuclear weapons during this entire period? Whatever the limits of conventional forces, could not the supply of atomic bombs keep the Soviet Union out of Western Europe? Churchill, whose speeches had moved Britons and Americans during the dark days of war, and who enjoyed turning phrases, liked to say during the postwar years that only the bomb stood between civilization and chaos—that, mirabile dictu, by a quirk of fate, the bad had preserved the good, the threat had made straight the way to safety. It was a paradoxical thing, the stuff of speeches, and Churchill could turn the logic a bit by pointing out the fragile nature of the arrangement and how it was necessary to rearm in a conventional way. In early 1947 he stirred Western Europe and some Americans and the result was the Council of Europe, where there was a forum but, frankly, not much more. That was another issue. Meanwhile, the atomic bomb preserved everything.

As years have passed, information has become available. Scholars have used it, and disquieting facts have emerged. One is the lack of bomb assembly teams during the first years of 1945–1950. When the army's control of nuclear weapons, including their manufacture, ended in January 1947 with organization of the Atomic Energy Commission (AEC), the bomb assembly teams that the army had brought together and trained were dispersed. As David A. Rosenberg has shown, throughout the rest of that year the AEC had no teams. To put together a bomb was complicated, requiring twenty-four men and nearly two days. Then, because of the need to recharge a weapon's batteries, the bomb could not remain in a plane for more than forty-eight hours. Moreover, the polonium initiators necessary to ready a critical mass, a vital part of the bomb, had a half-life of 138 days and were in short supply in 1947. What would have happened in an emergency during 1947? This was the year of decision with the Soviet Union, with the Truman Doctrine and the Marshall Plan. During that time the United States possessed almost no nuclear weapons.[4] At the outset of 1947 there might have been, after assembly, a single bomb. Years later Gregg Herken spoke with the first chairman of the AEC, Lilienthal, who remembered that he had gone to Los Alamos to look over the weapons laboratory and storage facilities. "Probably one of the saddest days of my life was to walk down in that chicken-wire enclosure. They weren't even protected, what gimmicks there were. . . . I was shocked when I found out . . . Actually we had one that was probably operable when I first went off to Los Alamos, one that had a good chance of being operable." That was close to the total, if perhaps a bit low. Truman in a horrendous breach of security told White House staffers in 1946 that the United States had six bombs. In another breach in 1947 he told one of his World War I lieutenants, visiting at the White House, that the country had eleven.[5]

In regard to numbers, in subsequent years there was encouraging and discouraging news. Beginning in 1948 production rose rapidly. An arrangement with Britain and Canada, concluded in January 1948, gave the United States the entire production of uranium in the Belgian Congo. Fat Boy plutonium bombs, known as Mark III weapons, were being replaced by Mark IV bombs that used only half the plutonium and weapons-grade uranium. Mark III weapons required artisans; they were tailor-made. Mark IV bombs meant assembly lines. All the while, the AEC recruited assembly teams, and presumably the problem of the initiators was solved. The discouraging news was that the British physicist Klaus Fuchs, whom the FBI discovered was a spy, might have revealed to the Soviets the nature of the radar fusing mechanisms of the Fat Boy plutonium bombs. Until AEC scientists could replace the Fat Boys with Mark IVs, the Soviets could have jammed the aiming mechanisms of the bombs—all of the U.S. arsenal from 1945 until 1948. During those years the Soviets were fascinated with radar jamming, perhaps with reason.[6]

Nor was this plus-and-minus aspect of nuclear weapons everything that needs to be said about nuclear power in 1945–1950, for until the Korean War the Strategic Air Command (SAC) was incapable of dropping bombs on targets, even if the Soviets had not compromised the radar fusing mechanisms. The demobilization of 1945–1946 gravely affected the readiness of SAC. During the next two years the command was under the nominal guidance of Gen. George C. Kenney, a well-known figure during World War II, but the effective commander was Major General Clements McMullen, who reduced SAC's readiness to a shambles through a program known as cross-training, which required pilots to be competent in nonflying duties and crew members to learn alternate aircrew positions. McMullen trained his crews on targets that were easy compared with what would occur under combat conditions.

Planes flew at ten or fifteen thousand feet. In January 1949, SAC's new commander, the vigorous General Curtis E. LeMay, sent all his bomb groups over Dayton, Ohio, near Wright Field, in a simulated attack. He gave the crews maps of Dayton dated from 1938, required them to make passes at high altitude, and sent them in at night. The weather was poor, with thunderstorms. The result was a fiasco. Not a single plane fulfilled its mission. LeMay was so shaken by the bomb runs that he described the night as the darkest in Air Force history. During the next months he worked over his command, changed everything, and gradually matters came under control, but it is safe to say that not until 1950 was SAC able to do anything near what it was supposed to do.[7]

For more than sixty years, books and articles have appeared about the cold war, especially its beginnings in 1945–1950. In 1965 and after they turned to the inadequacies, though not always in detail, of President Truman and Secretaries Stettinius and Byrnes, and occasionally remarked on the confusion of the American people. Not many mentioned the lack of conventional force behind that era's diplomacy, and few remarked the possibility that the nuclear shield was anything but that. During this time, American military authorities were drawing up war plans, arranging how conventional and nuclear forces were to perform their allotted tasks. The Pentagon was full of ranking officers, rotated in and out, who drew up plans with such names as Pincher, Makefast, Broiler, Halfmoon, and Offtackle. Behind their projections was not very much— maybe nothing. On the Soviet side a good deal of this weakness must have been known. Verne W. Newton has shown the extraordinary successes of the British diplomat Donald Maclean, who penetrated the State Department and the AEC while his colleague Kim Philby did the same with the CIA.[8] What held off the Soviets, persuading them not to move while the advantage was on their side, is at present difficult to say.

President Franklin Delano Roosevelt's coffin is placed in the hearse. National Park Service—Abbie Rowe. Courtesy Harry S. Truman Library.

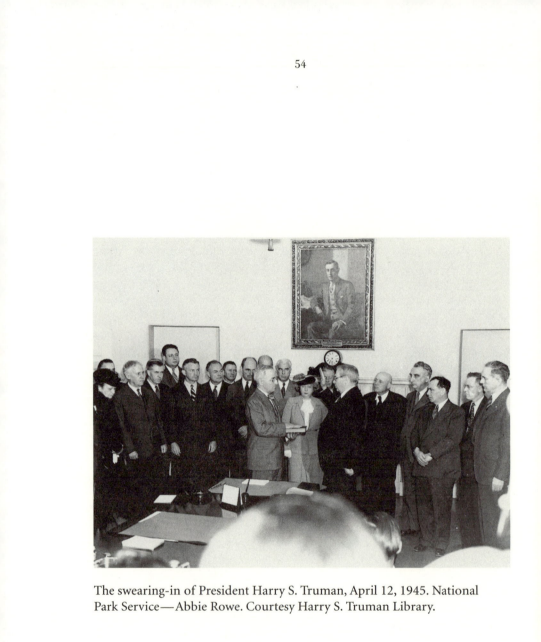

The swearing-in of President Harry S. Truman, April 12, 1945. National Park Service—Abbie Rowe. Courtesy Harry S. Truman Library.

Pennsylvania Avenue in front of the White House, at the time of the Japanese surrender, August 14, 1945. National Park Service—Abbie Rowe. Courtesy Harry S. Truman Library.

President Truman and Secretary of State George C. Marshall. National
Park Service—Abbie Rowe. Courtesy Harry S. Truman Library.

The B-36 bomber. Courtesy Harry S. Truman Library.

Ceremonies marked the arrival of the first Marshall Plan ship at Bordeaux, France. Courtesy Harry S. Truman Library.

President Truman waving from the back of his train on June 3, 1948. National Park Service—Abbie Rowe. Courtesy Harry S. Truman Library.

Truman and MacArthur at Wake Island. In thinking about the meeting later, the president took offense at the general's open shirt and sweat-soiled non-regulation cap. Department of State. Courtesy Harry S. Truman Library.

Lieutenant General Matthew B. Ridgway, who turned around the Korean War in December 1950–January 1951. Courtesy Harry S. Truman Library.

President Truman in retirement strolls on the square in Independence, Missouri. *St. Louis Post-Dispatch*. Courtesy Harry S. Truman Library.

FOUR

NATO

In spite of the frailty of judgments about contemporary history, it does seem that the North Atlantic Treaty changed the foreign policy of the United States beyond recall, ensuring the future—military, economic, political—of Western Europe. So one concludes from looking back over the more than fifty years of NATO's existence, overlooking the confusions, irritabilities, and even failures, the ups and downs that mark international affairs as surely as they beset individuals. Anyone old enough to remember the state of international affairs in the late 1940s can behold enormous change, indeed so much as to constitute a veritable revolution. One hesitates to use that word, hackneyed as it has become. Historians are fond of it. Still, it seems appropriate to describe the present, as against the now remote—and riddance to it—past after World War II, the opening years of the cold war.

Consider this revolution for what it has meant to aging students of contemporary history who remember the climactic last year of World War II in Europe, the dull thud of buzz bombs and V-2 rockets upon defenseless, broken-windowed London, and, across the Channel, the sirens on the tanks moving up the country roads of Normandy. After such experiences they wanted some sort of assurance that their nations would not make the same errors as after World War I. As it turned out, they were much surprised that upon defeating one foe in Europe it was necessary to confront another. They were not keen on a permanent American presence in Europe, but if such was necessary, they were for it. Fortunately, they thought, President Truman, Congress, and the American people took the essential measures. Almost 150 years before the revolutionary beginning in 1949, the American nation in the now-forgotten Treaty of Morfontaine had escaped from its first—and for a century and a half, only—alliance. With the North Atlantic Treaty there was again involvement, an enormous change, if one chose to think about it. As for Western Europeans, the treaty of 1949 gave hope to, and then substantial defense against, what was a dangerous situation; beginning with the Korean War the treaty led to a respectable, if never convincing, military balance with the forces of the Soviet Union. This allowed Western Europe's economic revival, initially through the Marshall Plan, in course by April 4, 1949, and commencing in the summer of 1950 through the huge offshore American purchases during the Korean War. The result, economically speaking, was revolutionary; in the words of Walt W. Rostow, Western Europe's economies "took off."[1] In the 1990s, the European Community nations were admiring the prospect of another takeoff. And Western Europe's economic miracle has helped reduce the Continent's political nationalism. It has played some part in bringing to power the regime in Russia that is breaking with the communist and tsarist past, with all such a regime can mean for European and world peace.

It is possible that history may make another turn, of 180 degrees, and go the wrong way, a veritable revolution in reverse. In international affairs such revolutions have occurred. Hugh R. Trevor-Roper pointed out the melancholy result of the Pacification of Ghent in 1576, as forgotten a moment as Morfontaine in 1800.[2] In the sixteenth century a great prince had seemed to triumph by uniting the Low Countries in favor of enlightened religion and, so far as concerned the burghers, even more enlightened commerce and manufacturing. According to the scheme of William of Orange, all Europe would look to Ghent as a beacon for its progress. Not for a moment would it be possible for the sovereign of Spain, Philip II, to challenge light with his regal darkness. But as Trevor-Roper told so well, history met defiance in the person of the Spanish monarch, whose advisers told him that by eliminating William of Orange, through assassination, much good would follow. All the monarchs and princes did it, the advisers said; a small sin could result in far greater good. William therefore passed to his heavenly reward, the Low Countries became a charnel house of war, and in the next century the Thirty Years War raised nationalism as the end-all of Europe, with war as its handmaiden, and doomed the Western world to three hundred years of darkness. Even the twentieth century, as John Lukacs has shown in a brilliant but, alas, unpublished essay, was a theater of nationalism, the curse of Philip II. It was rival nationalisms, not capitalism versus communism, that marked the international calamities of our time.

We nonetheless must take courage. Trevor-Roper's exposition is entrancing; this master essayist could set up his purposes and by analogy take his readers the way he wished them to go. The year 1576, he made us believe, was a point of change, a great moment, and history went the wrong way. But facing another moment in 1949, history surely went the right way, and may continue to do so.

1

A few years ago the author of a book on the United States Strategic Air Command during its initial years, including the period of the foundation of NATO in 1948–1949, wrote plaintively that before drawing the meaning of great international policies historians ought to look at the military hardware and the military technicians that were to take those policies into the realm of fact. Part of the problem, as Harry R. Borowski drew it, was that information on the Soviets was not forthcoming, and crucial American military records were not available until 1974.[3] Also part of the problem, perhaps, was the tendency of all of us to equate the ideal with the real, especially if it involved—as in Borowski's book—an organization led by a man who boasted about taking people back to the Stone Age. Similarly, it was tempting not to look at SAC because it dealt in hardware that all of us essentially disliked.

The truth is that the military position of the Western nations in 1945–1950 was appalling, and only at the end of the half decade was there the beginning of change—because of the Korean War's large increases in conventional armaments and, in nuclear arms, the Atomic Energy Commission's creation of bomb assembly teams, the changeover to Mark IV bombs, and General LeMay's reforms in SAC.

Beyond question the war plans of the Western European nations and of the United States were ambitious to a fault. If those on the American side had been carried out they would have placed an immediate foundation under what Melvyn P. Leffler has described as "the American conception of national security."[4] On both sides of the Atlantic, however, the staff statements of the time started resolutely and ended in doubletalk. They were English compositions and, in a sense, unworthy of the intelligent officers and their assistants who sat around tables fifty and more years ago. In reading the plans of the staffs, not merely those of the Brussels powers of 1948–1949 but also those of the joint chiefs of staff in Washington, one has the impression of generals and admirals, some of them principal figures in the recent war, sitting around highly varnished tables and talking of dreams—the troops, and the bombs and planes, were not in existence.

Perhaps the less said about Western European plans for defense the better, for those plans were crude in the extreme. Indeed, there were none until the time of the Brussels Pact. That is, there were none save for plans for evacuating the occupation troops from the Channel and the Pyrenees, if the occupation troops were able to get there after the Russian hordes started to move west.

But Brussels demanded plans, and the question became how far east the pact's forces could make a stand. At the beginning, and in the end, the decision was swathed in meaningless words, such as the plan communicated to Ambassador Lewis W. Douglas on May 14, 1948: "The five powers are now assessing their resources and fully recognize that an attack in the near future would find them militarily weak."[5] The plans did not move much beyond that point, although there was considerable discussion, with suitable expression of national interests, of who would command the nearly nonexistent troops. Here the French, who were supposed to contribute the largest forces to the Western European army (but possessed no equipment and already were harried by the requirements of Algeria and Indochina), were terribly concerned that they might be under command of the British, who undoubtedly would then produce a scheme to bring in West German troops of some sort. The five powers agreed to have a French army general, French admiral, and British air marshal placed in command. By this time discussions were proceeding for some sort of wider pact in which the United States would participate, and the Brussels powers suggested an American supreme commander. General Clay in Berlin thought of resigning if American troops went under command of a Brussels general. Washington advised him that it did "not want an American commander too closely associated with the overall initial debacle."[6]

In September 1948 the Western Union defense organization made Field Marshal Sir Bernard Montgomery chairman of the commanders-in-chief committee, with headquarters eventually at Fontainebleau. Montgomery, military-political schemer that he was, then got to work. According to an equally irrepressible American State Department official, Theodore Achilles, one of the earliest secret telegrams that "Monty" sent to the war office in London said, "My present instructions are to hold the line at the Rhine. Presently available allied forces might enable me to hold the tip of the Brittany peninsula for three days. Please instruct further." Montgomery also began to annoy the French by proposing a command setup modeled on that of the British and Americans during the Normandy invasion, namely, two army groups above the army corps organizations. The French knew that one group would be under American command and the other under British, with General Jean de Lattre de Tassigny becoming an errand boy to the corps commanders.[7]

While the Brussels nations in 1948 were playing with command problems and stating their essential problem in as many words as possible, the Americans in Washington were not doing much better. For the first three years after World War II the United States had no joint strategic plan, as a commission chaired by Thomas K. Finletter discovered late in 1947. The five members of the commission inquired as to whether a plan was available. Finletter went to Truman, who promised to obtain it.

Shortly afterward Admirals Leahy and Nimitz and Generals Dwight D. Eisenhower and Hoyt S. Vandenberg met with the Finletter group and presented the plan, "pages thick, pages and pages," accompanied by an oral exposition. The group found the briefing very confusing, and after several questions General Eisenhower apologized. "I'm sorry, I guess my mind is worse than I thought it was," he said. "I can't understand what the war plan is." After more discussion he continued, "Gentlemen, these five civilian gentlemen who are here are just patriotic American citizens trying to do something they've been asked to do by the President. I think we owe it to them to tell them that there is no war plan."[8]

In these years the services made do with such ad hoc plans as the Air Force–generated "Makefast," which hypothecated six B-29 groups operating from Cairo and England within four months of the opening of hostilities, and believed that such a force could destroy three-fourths of Russia's petroleum-producing capacity in nine months and destroy the mobility of Soviet ground and air forces in one year. The plan left open whether planes would carry nuclear or conventional bombs.[9] Two-thirds of the Soviet petroleum industry was in seventeen cities, and by July 1948 the joint chiefs came up with a "short-range emergency war plan," "Halfmoon," which called for dropping fifty atomic bombs on twenty cities important for petroleum and other items, in order to cause "paralysis of at least 50 percent of Soviet industry." Upon being briefed on May 5, President Truman ordered an alternate plan based on conventional bombing. The president thought the bomb might be outlawed by the time war came, through the Baruch Plan or some such arrangement. As the Berlin crisis deepened and turned into a blockade, with the Western airlift at first a chancy proposition, Truman reluctantly assured Secretary of Defense Forrestal that "if it became necessary" he might use nuclear weapons, and he endorsed NSC-30, a National Security Council document that looked in that direction. Halfmoon, incidentally, called for forces in Germany to withdraw to the Rhine ("but it is probable that U.S. forces will withdraw through France either to French coastal ports or to the Pyrenees") and envisioned SAC planes deploying to bases in England, Khartoum-Cairo-Suez, and Okinawa.[10]

But was it not true that behind the inability of the military staffs, foreign and domestic, to guarantee the safety of Western Europe by conventional means, there was a merciful if not a providential reliance on what the political scientist Bernard Brodie in a widely read book of the time described as "the ultimate weapon"? Certainly people in Western Europe and the United States believed that Western Europe's security rested ultimately with the atomic bombs carried by the U.S. Air Force's Strategic Air Command. So did officials, including even President Truman on occasion (he could wobble, as in his analysis of Halfmoon). On February 9, 1949, the president talked with the chairman of the Atomic Energy Commission, Lilienthal, who unknown to friends and acquaintances was keeping a massive diary. He recorded that Truman told him that "the atomic bomb was the mainstay and all he had; that the Russians would have probably taken over Europe a long time ago if it were not for that."[11]

The arresting fact of the West's reliance on the American SAC in the early postwar years was that it was entirely misplaced. Here the merciful or perhaps providential part was probably that the Russians did not know this. Forcing the American armed services into ever smaller budgets prior to the Korean War had so reduced conventional forces that only nuclear bombs could have saved the West. Yet even with the ultimate weapon—partly because of budget constraints, mainly because of very poor leadership—SAC was no reliance at all.

The budget question was only in lesser part the problem of SAC. When things changed for the better the necessity in terms of personnel was only an increase from 52,000 to 71,000 men, no large matter within a total armed forces strength of 1.5 million. The budget, to be sure, was tight, and for fiscal year 1950 (July 1, 1949, to June 30, 1950) the administration asked $14.4 billion and received $13.9 billion. But this was not too far from an acceptable budget, according to a man who should have known. General Eisenhower wrote in his diary for February 19, 1949, "I personally and very earnestly believe that $15 billion to $16 billion per year is all that this country need spend for security forces, if it is done every year (with some additional amounts to cover past deficits)."[12]

Most of the problem lay elsewhere, in leadership. And here the lesser part of the difficulty was in supervising production of fissionable material and fabrication of bombs. The stockpile, of course, was quite insufficient for the hopes placed upon it by the president and the State Department and Department of Defense, not to mention the European allies. David Alan Rosenberg first published the figures for 1945–1948, and Steven L. Rearden in his official history of the Defense Department has corroborated them, showing two weapons ready by late 1945, nine by June 30, 1946, thirteen by mid-1947, and fifty by mid-1948.[13] As Rosenberg also related, Forrestal and Nimitz provided recommendations on production rates of bombs; neither knew the size of the stockpile or the current rate of production, but each assumed the other did. Rosenberg has stressed, too, the necessary slowness in assembling bombs, the short time that a bomb could remain within an aircraft, and the manner in which the life of workable bombs was limited by the polonium initiators.

SAC's worst problem was its bumbling leadership, until LeMay took over in October 1948. Such is the conclusion of Borowski, who made an exhaustive study of SAC's difficulties. The command's ineptitude may have derived from the Air Force's straining to become independent, which took so much of the energy of its leaders. SAC's first commander was General Kenney, who was a good speaker and spent a great deal of time giving Air Force speeches around the country. The Air Force's first chief of staff, General Carl Spaatz, may have been doing much the same thing. Whatever the reason, this left SAC's deputy commander, McMullen, as the architect of many of the problems that plagued the command until LeMay took over.

To recite—in an essay dedicated to the origins of NATO—the problems of General McMullen is to go into too much detail. Suffice it to say that the foundation of Western military retaliation rested with this virtually unknown general, who through cross-training nearly reduced the Western world's defenses to a shambles. He also thought that to cut staffs would make the boys more efficient. His motto was "Give them half of what they asked for, work them twice as hard, and they will get twice as much done."

The air force realized that the quickest route to the Soviet Union lay over the North Pole, and thus the best course was to put bomb groups on Ladd Field near Fairbanks. But there the men found what it was like to fly in appallingly cold weather, when even to start the engines was an experience of hours, and then how hard it was to get the planes to stay up when lines were freezing. Moreover, they were fearful of becoming lost. "If one were to remove that portion of the globe north of the Arctic Circle and position it over the geographical center of the United States, it would cover the entire nation, Mexico, most of Cuba, large portions of the Pacific and Atlantic Oceans, and nearly all of the Canadian provinces."[14] If a flier bailed out he would not last long, and if he went down on the polar ice cap or in the area of continual winter darkness he would have only time enough to say his prayers.

Other problems arose, such as the "silverplating" of the B-29s. This involved much more than strengthening frames and opening up wide hatches for the five-ton Fat Boy bombs of the time, the plutonium bombs of Alamogordo and Nagasaki. By the end of 1946 only about half of the forty-six so-modified planes remained from the recent war. To silverplate each new plane required six thousand hours.

Then there was the business of getting a bomb on target, which, as we have seen, LeMay discovered his predecessors had virtually ignored.[15]

The weakness of Western forces at this time was drawn in stark terms at a meeting of NATO foreign ministers with the highest American officials—President Truman, Secretary of State Acheson, Secretary of Defense Louis Johnson (who replaced Forrestal)—on the evening before the treaty was signed, April 3, 1949. A stenographic account of the meeting, incidentally, came to light in the Truman Library. Only Lawrence S. Kaplan, the indefatigable NATO researcher, had seen this document before its reappearance.[16] During that outspoken session, with no outsiders present, Secretary Johnson said "neither the signing of the Atlantic pact nor any initial U.S. military aid program is going to enable us to hold the Rhine line. It will be some years, assuming continued U.S. aid and probably increasing rearmament by Western Europe itself, before we can feel confident of our ability to do this." The president was no more comforting, and in one respect less. "We must not close our eyes to the fact that, despite the huge U.S. war potential, the Western nations are practically disarmed and have no power sufficient to prevent the five hundred Soviet divisions from overrunning Western Europe and most of Asia. To be sure, we have the atomic bomb; but we must recognize the present limitations of our strategic methods for delivering it."[17]

2

In the American system of government the president of the United States sits in his office in the west wing of the White House and presides, as his title indicates, over the work of his subordinates. But that is what the Constitution of the eighteenth century prescribed, and from the outset there were great practical differences from the written document. One might have thought that Secretary of Defense Forrestal was at least presiding over his sprawling cabinet office, but that was not true. One day when President Truman's naval aide, Rear Admiral Robert L. Dennison, was in the oval office, Truman looked at him owlishly through his thick glasses and said, "Do you know who the secretary of defense is?"

Dennison played along with the president and said, "Yes, sir, Jim Forrestal."

"You're wrong," was the response. "*I'm* the secretary of defense. Jim calls me up several times a day asking me to make a decision on matters that are completely within his competence, but he passes them on to me."[18]

One can only be thankful that Truman, who had an acute sense of how to run the government of the United States and possessed an essentially civilian point of view, presided over civil-military relations in the early postwar years. In 1948, Forrestal wanted the military to have possession of the atomic bombs, and Truman would have none of it. Perhaps it made no difference, for the military could not have dropped them on targets if they had them.

In the commonsense way that the government worked during the Truman administration, the president was assisted by two excellent secretaries of state, whose qualities were epitomized in a remark by Acheson to the historian Gaddis Smith. General Marshall once told Acheson there were two kinds of men: those who dealt with action and those who dealt with description. Acheson was no man to hide his light and added: "He [Marshall] was entirely the former. I have been both."[19]

Truman, Marshall, and Acheson had plenty to be levelheaded about, whether active, descriptive, or both, during the years 1948–1949 when the North Atlantic Treaty took shape. In the developing historiography of the cold war, Leffler has written that there were no real fears of Russian conquest, that year after year the intelligence agencies predicted no Russian attack, but the American military, aided and abetted by the president and his State Department assistants, listened to the accounts of capability, countered them with economic and military programs, and created the strained relations with the Soviet Union they said they hoped to avoid.[20] Still, there were scares, real war scares. Regarding General Clay's cable of March 5, 1948, when Clay for the first time thought war was possible. Leffler relates that Clay was trying for increased defense expenditures. A State Department memorandum of the same date showed, on an attached note in Truman's hand, that the president was uneasy. Truman listed trouble spots beginning with Turkey and Greece and asked, "Shall we state the case to the Congress, name names and call the turn? Will Russia move first? Who pulls the trigger?" There followed other worried moments for a man as unflappable as Truman. September 13, 1948: "Have a terrific day. Forrestal, Bradley, Vandenberg (the general, not the senator), [Stuart] Symington brief me on the bases, bombs, Moscow, Leningrad, etc. I have a terrible feeling afterward that we are very close to war. I hope not. Discuss situation with Marshall at lunch." Nearly a year later, on August 31, 1949, after the North Atlantic Treaty had been signed and the organization was under way, there was another scare; during the president's staff meeting he told the group the country was nearer war than it had been at any time—this over the Russians' contention with the Yugoslav government of Tito. On this occasion he added that the United States had few arms.[21]

The North Atlantic Treaty was drawn up in 1948, a year of crises, especially at its outset—the Czech coup of February, by which Czechoslovakia lost its independence, followed by the death of Masaryk, and the rapid worsening of relations with the Soviets that resulted in the Berlin blockade in June. In autumn, matters seemed to straighten out, with a peace offensive on the part of the Soviets (less pressure through communist parties in France and Italy and failure to place heavy demands on Finland and Norway, as had been expected). Statesmen could hardly take comfort, however, in what they assumed to be only a lull. It is instructive that the second secretary of the British embassy in Washington, Maclean, attended early meetings of the Western nations looking to formation of NATO. He must have sent word that the Washington deliberations were altogether pacific and defensive. The West had no mole in the Kremlin.

The man who got treaty negotiations going, beyond doubt, was the foreign secretary of Britain, Bevin, who spoke with Marshall just after the failure of the first London Conference in December 1947—the conference that was supposed to settle the German problem but succumbed to a series of intransigences perpetrated by Molotov. Bevin acted, even though the omens for his being an agent of change were hardly good. At the conference's end Marshall had worked out an arrangement whereby he and Bevin would cooperate in breaking up the meetings, but Bevin, through sheer fumbling, Acheson later thought, failed on his part of the bargain, and Marshall had to do it himself. As for Truman, he confidentially believed Bevin a boor and, more to the point, an SOB, perhaps because Bevin had spoken openly of Truman's Palestine policy. But Bevin was responsible for initiating negotiations for the North Atlantic Treaty; he invited Marshall to a private dinner that the secretary of state thought was a social event and began to talk unintelligibly about two circles. As soon as Marshall got back to his hotel he told his assistant, John D. Hickerson, "I wasn't prepared for it. If I had known he was going to talk about this I would have taken you down. You've got to go down and see what the guy has in mind." Bevin was talking about negotiation for the Brussels Pact, which was one circle, a tight one, and he wanted another circle, not as tightly drawn, that would include the United States and Canada.[22]

What happened thereafter is well known. Bevin made a speech in the House of Commons in January 1948, and the British ambassador in Washington asked for talks, which began in Washington.

In all this Bevin was helped by former Prime Minister Churchill, whose favorite line of verse was "Westward look the land is bright."[23] Churchill was championing what became the Council of Europe, an idealistic organization with no powers to which nations sent representatives. Bevin thought that organization useless, and dangerous, and in his cockney accent made one of his best remarks about the danger: "If you open that Pandora's box you never know what Trojan 'orses will jump out." Churchill, meanwhile, was muddying the waters by advising his American cousins to tell off the Russians ("tell the Soviets that if they do not retire from Berlin and abandon Eastern Germany, with-drawing to the Polish frontier, we will raze their cities").[24] Nonetheless, the former prime minister's more sensible agitations helped Bevin's more sensible proposal.

Once conversations began, the details were pretty much up to the Americans, for the Brussels Pact powers needed American power and the price would have to be paid mostly by the giver, despite the talk on both sides about mutuality. Bevin did not care what form association of the United States with Western Europe took, so long as there was a presence.

As it turned out, some American officials were helpful and some were not. Hickerson and his associate in the State Department, Achilles, were ringleaders in pushing through a form of agreement that would work. After Marshall sent him over to talk to Foreign Office officials about the two circles, Hickerson jumped at the possibility of extending the Brussels Pact. He took ship back to the United States with the Republi-can delegate to the London Conference, John Foster Dulles, and con-verted Dulles to the project. Fortifying himself with fish-house punch on New Year's Eve 1948, he told Achilles, "I don't care whether entangling alliances have been considered worse than original sin ever since George Washington's time. We've got to negotiate a military alliance with West-ern Europe in peacetime and we've got to do it quickly." There followed committee meetings and "ulcer lunches of stale sandwiches or gummy beans from the scruffy newsstand snack bar across the hall," and the working group came up with a draft treaty, ready by the beginning of September.[25]

In the arrangement of the treaty, Hickerson may have been the de-signer, and he was so designated by Achilles. At the outset he wanted the Brussels Pact, which was being negotiated in February, directed gen-erally, at an unspecified enemy, not at Germany as was the Dunkirk Treaty of 1947. He suggested the formula of the Rio Treaty of inter-American cooperation (1947): an attack against one would be an attack against all, each nation choosing weapons according to its constitutional processes. Undersecretary of State Robert A. Lovett—for weeks at a time Secretary Marshall was out of the country attending international conferences—did not want to do that and said, "I don't think we had ought to do this. Let's just give it our blessing." Hickerson said he felt strongly. Marshall, a good staff man, gave Lovett's draft his blessing, but said, "Now, give this back to Hickerson. He feels strongly. Tell him to call in the British ambassador and give him all this [Hickerson's suggestion] orally, but on the record this [the blessing] is all we've done." Hickerson sent for Lord Inverchapel and gave him the signed note and said, "Now here is the note *I* wanted to send, and I'm authorized by the secretary to let you see this." After reading the note aloud Hickerson added a sly explanation: "If your memory were perfect you could memorize that, so I'll just give you a copy of it. It has no status except to refresh your memory. . . . in your memorandum of conversation you may quote this."[26]

Curiously, the two senior department people one might have thought would have taken the lead with ideas and action—and they were talented with the former—did little to advance the North Atlantic Treaty. The counselor of the department, Charles E. Bohlen, believed that military aid would suffice and that a treaty would only get in trouble with the Senate. The head of the policy planning staff, Kennan, talked about a dumbbell arrangement, with the U.S. and Canada and perhaps Britain on one end and the Europeans on the other. Sometimes he looked in the direction of Europe as a third force, an approach that later was known as disengagement. John Gaddis has drawn their ideas in terms of a paradox: in 1945, Bohlen had favored a third force, and Kennan a sphere of influence; by the time of negotiation of NATO they had changed positions. Bohlen, Gaddis contends, reflected the mainstream of thinking in Washington; Kennan, as so often, was the outsider. The truth may be that both of these department idea men found NATO uninteresting, perhaps because it was not a clear-cut arrangement.[27]

In negotiations in Washington and Europe in 1948 the positions taken regarding non–Brussels Pact nations were sometimes piquant and always interesting. In the former category was a conversation that Marshall had with Foreign Minister Bo Osten Undén of Sweden, who took advantage of the secretary's presence in Paris in October to explain Sweden's traditional neutrality, which by that time, Undén said, had lasted 135 years. Even during the Soviet-Finnish war the Swedes were virtuously neutral, and the Russians appreciated that, as well they might have. Relations with the Soviets at the moment were good. He feared that any move by Sweden to ally with the West might affect Finland, which the Russians were leaving alone. Marshall said that there had been a feeling of neutrality in the United States, and he inquired what the effect might have been if Presidents Woodrow Wilson and Franklin Roosevelt had maintained such a policy. Undén admitted it would have been tragic but said that the United States was a great power. Marshall retorted that the United States among almost all the other countries of the world could best afford from its own selfish security point of view to be neutral. Undén said that Sweden was like Switzerland; Marshall said there was a considerable difference geographically. Toward the end Undén made the comment that the problem of Swedish neutrality, 135 years of it, was his problem. Marshall agreed but said that as Undén had spoken frankly, so he, Marshall, had sought to speak.[28]

Italy desired an invitation to join the Atlantic treaty. The Americans refused until the Italians—whose military contribution might be less than nothing—asked for an invitation. Involved in their inquiry was their need (since they would be inquiring) not to mention territorial ambitions in Africa. The Portuguese government, an embarrassment under the conservative guidance of Antonio de Oliveira Salazar, at first sniffed and talked about the exclusion of Franco Spain, but then asked to be included.

Canada contributed Article 2 of the treaty, the Canadian article, which Acheson described as the "pie in the sky" article. Because the French Canadians in Quebec would not desire commitments that were exclusively military, the Canadian government wanted an article that would look toward an Atlantic community. Achilles later discussed with the Canadian diplomat Escott Reid, by that time out of the Canadian foreign service, the obstacles to Article 2 that Reid espied and Achilles did not see, obstacles that the persistent Canadians overcame. Both Reid and the then undersecretary (later secretary) for foreign affairs, Lester B. Pearson, took a feeling of considerable accomplishment from Article 2.[29]

It remained to use special care with the Senate, which in 1948 was a part of the famous or (according to President Truman on the electoral

circuit) infamous Eightieth Congress. There was no Democratic majority in the Senate. Moreover, it was necessary to take care with the American people who, like the Republican senators, were concerned about
interference of the treaty with the American Constitution and with the
United Nations Charter. The constitutional problem required preserving the right of Congress to consent to a declaration of war. The UN
problem required attention to Articles 51, 53, and 54 of the charter.
The former difficulty was resolved by fuzzing the terms of decision
over how to repel an attack, which for Europeans lost the pointedness
of the Brussels Pact article that set out the mechanics of decision. Here
the opinion of Bevin, that the form was unimportant so long as the
engagement was made, proved wise. As for the decision to establish an
organization in accord with Article 51 of the charter, a regional organization, that was impossible to reconcile with Articles 53 and 54, which
required authorization of (53) and information to (54) the UN Security Council. As Kaplan has written, "The North Atlantic Treaty could
meet neither requirement."[30] Russia was a permanent member of the
Security Council. This, however, was no more quixotic an arrangement
(to stress one article that conflicted with two others) than the fact that
the North Atlantic Treaty had arisen directly because the United Nations Organization had proved almost a failure as a result of the veto
power—the Soviet vetoes. Americans had forgotten that, at the San
Francisco Conference in 1945, Senator Tom Connally had demanded
that the charter give each permanent member of the Security Council a
veto. Before the members of one of the conference's committees he had
said, "If you want a charter, you can have a charter with the veto or no
charter at all," whereupon he tore up a copy of the charter.[31]

For the Truman administration one of the most difficult tasks might
have been getting the nearly revolutionary treaty (with its confusions
over constitutional process and over three articles of the charter) through
the Senate, where unfriendly senators and their constituents might have
a field day. For this purpose the president and Secretary Marshall dele-
gated Undersecretary Lovett, a man of infinite patience and subtlety,
which he needed for the task. Lovett had to deal with Senator Vandenberg, whom Acheson later credited with the intellectual necessity of
opposing any suggestion from a Democratic administration or even a

rival politician of his own party, then undergoing a conversion and thereafter arranging a resurrection of the perverse suggestion in the form of a Vandenberg Resolution.[32] Lovett spent hours in what were known as "500 G" meetings—500 G being Vandenberg's suite at the Wardman Park Hotel. The essence of the negotiation appeared one day when Lovett ventured the possibility of a presidential declaration of willingness to negotiate a treaty. He was met with a resounding "No!" "Why," asked Vandenberg, "should Truman get all the credit?"[33] The senator introduced his own resolution, which the Senate adopted on June 11, 1948, in a vote of 64 to 4.

3

When the treaty was signed on April 4, 1949, relations between the signatories and the Union of Soviet Socialist Republics had settled down from the fears and, apparently, confusions of the year before. It is fair to describe April 1949 as a poised moment, much like the Geneva summit meeting in 1955. Everything appeared to be going the way of the West. Fighting had resumed in Greece between government and communist forces, but this time the government gained the upper hand, and for all practical purposes, mainly because of Tito's defection from Moscow, the trouble in Greece was over. By this time the Berlin blockade was about to end, made ineffective by the airlift. Truman had been elected and no longer was subject to slighting remarks that he was an accidental president. The new secretary of state, Acheson, was a strong successor to Secretary Marshall. In the Attlee cabinet Bevin held an unassailable position, as in pushing for the treaty he had triumphed over the perhaps indifference, and certainly the Commonwealth preferences, of his chief, the prime minister.[34]

The strategic picture in the North Atlantic area was clouded, but there was hope. The United States and its allies could rely neither on nuclear protection nor on protection by conventional military force. Fortunately, on both levels, the picture was about to improve.

It is true that during the entire period of the cold war NATO had to rely mainly on the threat of nuclear force to preserve itself against the

Soviet Union. The nuclear turnaround came quickly in the years after 1949. There was a change in the nature of weapons. The Truman administration undertook development of the H-bomb, a weapon of mass destruction, for it could not be aimed. This was a bothersome move, but necessary, for otherwise the American nation could have been threatened at will by the Soviet Union if the USSR alone had developed an H-bomb. The Soviets began this spiral of bomb development by exploding a nuclear device on August 29, 1949. They had managed through espionage to obtain the design of the Nagasaki plutonium bomb and duplicated it. On January 11, 1950, Truman arranged a meeting of a three-man advisory committee, consisting of Secretaries Johnson and Acheson and Chairman Lilienthal of the Atomic Energy Commission. When Lilienthal attempted to hold out against development of the "super," Truman cut him off in the middle of his exposition, saying that he, the president, had no alternative. He announced his decision, and it was released to the press that evening.[35]

Truman did not like the new weapon but had to tolerate it. He never was the ardent supporter of weapons that his critics beheld, a sort of antediluvian character who sat behind the desk in the oval office and grinned as he signed appropriations for the AEC. Shortly before he left office in 1953 he responded to a letter from a member of the AEC, Thomas E. Murray, who wrote that it was an error to make nuclear issues stand apart from other issues of warfare. "I rather think you have put a wrong construction on my approach to the use of the Atomic bomb. It is far worse than gas and biological warfare because it affects the civilian population and murders them by the wholesale." He accepted such weapons with intense reluctance.[36]

At the same time the H-bomb was developed, the SAC under LeMay became efficient. By 1950 the command was using a new kind of aerial refueling, exchanging a difficult hose-and-reel system for a relatively easy flying boom. It was operating 225 nuclear-bomb-carrying aircraft, including silver-plated B-29s, B-50s (which were B-29s built for longer range and for carrying nuclear bombs), and thirty-four of the new and huge B-36s. The last were outmoded before they came in, as the design had been drawn in 1941 when it appeared that Britain might go under, unable to resist the Luftwaffe, and America needed a plane that could bomb Germany from North American bases. The B-36s were to last only a few years, until the B-52s—those venerables of the air that are still flying—came along in 1953–1954. Possessing six huge propeller-driven engines, the B-36s towered over their predecessors and successors—in the air force museum at Wright-Patterson Field near Dayton the prize exhibit is the B-36, which spreads its wings across a hangar the size of a football field, covering the motley collection of other planes. With this plane and its smaller cousins, LeMay had readied 263 combat crews by 1950 and was training 49 more. He had eighteen bomb-assembly teams and was adding four. He was flying his bomb groups over Baltimore, a city that resembled Soviet targets.[37]

Meanwhile, there was hope for the development of a conventional military force. For a while the theoretical strategic plans had to continue. The assumption of "Offtackle," the plan approved by the American joint chiefs in December 1949, was that the Soviets would overrun West Germany. "While the countries which have signed the Atlantic Pact will have improved economically and militarily, they will be unable, with the exception of the United Kingdom, to effectively resist being overrun and occupied by Soviet forces." The plan envisaged holding a substantial bridgehead in Western Europe, or if this was infeasible, the earliest practical return of troops, in order, as the document explained, "to prevent the exploitation and Communization of that area with long-term disastrous effects on U.S. national interests."[38] But the hope in the conventional arms picture was not Offtackle, one more high school essay by the joint chiefs, but another essay that promised something for Europe, the medium-term defense plan to be completed in phases by 1954. It did not merely promise a stand at the Rhine, as Montgomery hoped in 1948, but anticipated shifting supply lines and national responsibilities. It projected ninety ready and reserve divisions and a tactical air force of eight thousand planes. "Charade though the medium-term defense plan may have been," Kaplan has written, "it checked the deterioration of morale which had greeted the short-term program" of cut and run.[39]

The medium-term plan became the basis for military aid, to which Congress gave consent after some hesitation. The day after the North Atlantic Treaty was signed, on April 5, the Brussels Pact countries announced arms requests, and the United States responded the next day. The administration request was for $1.45 billion for foreign military aid, and two-thirds of the money was to go to NATO countries. By this time the political complexion of Congress had changed: the Eighty-first Congress was Democratic, and Vandenberg's role as leading man in the Foreign Relations Committee had come to an end, with replacement by the equally histrionic Connally. Not about to be taken from the stage, Vandenberg led a revolt against arms grants, against "the war lord bill which would have made the President the top military dictator of all time." He said he preferred resort to the United Nations rather than passage of the Mutual Defense Assistance Program. After the Soviet Union detonated a nuclear device, Vandenberg underwent a conversion, and on October 6 Truman signed the act for $1.3 billion, with $1 billion for Europe. Its effect was slow and not too sure, for the European allies needed far more than the act allowed. But it was a start. By June 30, 1950, the president had obligated most of the 1949–1950 military aid funds, although only $49.3 million had been expended. Moreover, and unlike the Marshall Plan, military assistance promised to go on indefinitely.[40]

NATO admittedly was plagued by gigantism. The Americans, it often has been said, are prone to overorganization, and there was some of it in NATO, the attachment of an "O" to the North Atlantic Treaty. The attachment was diplomatic and military. Diplomatically it included a council and defense committee that set up a military committee (with a standing group representing the United States, Britain, and France). The council in May 1950 established a council of deputies "to meet in continuous session in London," a full-time body of "highly qualified persons."[41] Appearance of the Americans was not unwelcome to the French, for the Americans balanced off the British, who wanted to dominate the Brussels group but contribute no troops (not until March 1950 did the cabinet consent to reinforce its continental occupation force upon outbreak of war). A chance development then helped. When de Lattre de Tassigny went to Indochina as high commissioner in December 1950, General Eisenhower was appointed supreme commander. To the irritation of de Lattre de Tassigny's assistant, André Beaufre, this led to even more overorganization, "submitting to the cumbersome

American administrative machinery, which perceives organization only in the form of highly complex diagrams." The "period of painstaking craftsmanship," as Beaufre described the perception of his chief, had ended, and "though the armed forces could be built up only slowly and in a limited way, a torrent of staffs and departments suddenly appeared which in themselves equaled the effective forces of a good army."[42]

NATO nonetheless represented a great change in American foreign policy, "the American Revolution of 1949," in the words of one of its supporters. It also represented a marked change in the fortunes of Western Europe. On the western side of the Atlantic there was the obvious conversion of Americans to the belief that the country could not remain apart from the world, that alliances were essential, and that alliance with Western Europe was the most essential (as Vandenberg, with his instinct for obfuscation, would have said). Asked on the evening of April 3, 1949, during the session of the foreign ministers with American officials, whether Western Europe was the center of American attention, Secretary Johnson responded, "Absolutely."[43] On the European side, NATO gave courage at a time of need.

It constituted a lasting organization. The Rio Pact, NATO's prototype, never placed the "O" in its acronym, and indeed never had an acronym. SEATO and CENTO, the Southeast Asia Treaty Organization (to protect small countries in that area) and the Central Treaty Organization (to keep the Soviet Union out of the Middle East) disappeared in 1977 and 1979, respectively. NATO has functioned much better than the two principal supranational organizations of the last century: compared with the United Nations, which has shown continual signs of failure, NATO looks good; compared with the old League of Nations it looks even better, for President Woodrow Wilson's ideas about Europe were vague and insubstantial and probably never could have worked, even with American presence, Anglo-French agreement, German goodwill, and Soviet cooperation rather than idealistic hectoring. As mentioned at the outset, it is possible to testify for NATO in terms of economics alone—the benefits of a respite from fear of a Soviet occupation.

The detractors of NATO will always be with us. They are an unavoidable part of the baggage of change. The British historian Peter Foot has written that NATO was a scheme for European integration, "security on the cheap," so Americans could take their aid dollars elsewhere.[44] This was a plausible explanation, although the historian offered few proofs other than what he styled "perceptions" of the American mood, including what Americans might describe as humbuggery, such as congressional resolutions and other such effusions. David P. Calleo, a trenchant writer about the Atlantic economy, described NATO as providing "hegemony on the cheap" and said that the era of need had ended, and the Europeans could take up the burden. His view, widely shared in a time of American budget deficits, sounds like neoisolationism, although Calleo is too sophisticated to subscribe to that.

Agreeable change is not really what critics like. They never desire the moment ("jam tomorrow, and jam yesterday"). One should also inquire how they would have felt about a United States that turned in upon itself, or sought to draw a Monroe Doctrine line around the Western Hemisphere, with Europe succumbing.

All in all, it is difficult to think of a single international instrument that accomplished as much as NATO in such a short time, for so little money, for so many of America's friends.

FIVE

Truman and Korea

Many years have passed since the end of the Korean War, more than half a century since it began, and the veterans of that war are mostly in retirement from whatever civilian tasks they thereafter pursued. Those who remained in the army are similarly in retirement, meeting their former comrades in Florida or Arizona. Most Americans today were born after the end of the Korean War. One can say with assurance that memory of the war has dimmed markedly.

There is something else about the Korean War that is of more moment than the passage of time, and that is the querulousness with which so many people in our country react when the subject of the war in Korea comes up. They almost always remark their uncertainty about the war, and sometimes in opinionated fashion say it was Mr. Truman's War and, in any case, a war that did not accomplish much.

The dimming of memory and the coming of uncertainty seem a pity, in view of what the war stood for: it was a "good war," similar to American participation in World War II. The need to protect a weak nation, South Korea, should have been obvious from the beginning, both for the sake of the people of that new country and for reasons of American security in the Far East and in Europe. If aggression had succeeded it would have destroyed the American strategic position in East Asia and threatened it in Western Europe where the great measures of 1947–1949 were about to have an effect. Too, the Truman administration, contrary to the desire of General MacArthur, refused to resort to unconventional weapons—that is, the atomic bomb—and this noble restraint well showed how Americans felt about the use of such weapons, that they were suitable only in an extremity.

1

The first sign that a Korean War might take place was hardly visible when at the end of World War II in East Asia it was necessary to occupy the myriad territories of the Greater East Asia Co-Prosperity Sphere, sometimes known as the Eight Corners of the Universe under One Roof. It was necessary to divide Korea between American and Russian occupying forces. In a very short time, a matter of hours, two U.S. Army colonels, one of whom was a future secretary of state, Dean Rusk, did the job. Everything considered, they did well. They opted for a line, the thirty-eighth parallel, that was roughly at Korea's fifty-yard line, with more people and less industry in the south, the opposite in the north. Moreover, the line lay above the nation's capital, Seoul. If anything, the territory to be occupied by the Americans was more ambitious than the ability of the U.S. Army warranted, for troops had to be put in by ship, which would take time.

Once the dividing line was accepted by both countries, the cold war did the rest, ensuring a divided Korean nation. At the Moscow meeting of foreign ministers, the Soviet Union, the United States, and Great Britain sponsored a joint commission to bring about economic unification and a provisional government. The commission became a cipher because of the cold war, and the United States turned to the United Nations General Assembly, which accepted a plan of unification through a national election. The Soviets refused to allow a vote in their portion of the country; the vote below the parallel therefore created a Republic of Korea that the United States recognized in 1948.

The manner in which a temporary dividing line became the border of an independent nation was disheartening to the American government, and so was another and much larger event to the north of Korea, namely the collapse of the Chinese Nationalist government and the triumph of the People's Republic. It is a curious fact that if the Americans had managed to prop up the Nationalists, somehow, the Korean War probably would not have occurred. Or if it had, as a result of a civil war between North and South Korea, the U.S. Army could have unified Korea without fear of Chinese intervention. Unfortunately, such military advice as Americans proffered the Nationalist Chinese was utterly wasted. Major General David G. Barr reported in 1948, when the Nationalists had lost virtually everything except a refuge on the island of Formosa, that "no battle has been lost since my arrival due to lack of ammunition or equipment. Their [the Nationalists'] military debacles in my opinion can all be attributed to the world's worst leadership and many other morale destroying factors that led to a complete loss of will to fight."[1] The regime of General Chiang Kai-shek did not really want American advice. Nor, after perhaps some hesitation, did Chiang's adversaries, the Communists. In fact there was a very considerable dislike of Americans on both sides of the Chinese struggle, and for that reason alone any major intervention by the United States would have achieved no more result than did remaining apart from the huge conflict. General Marshall, who sought futilely to bring the two sides together during most of 1946, described the difficulties in China when he said, "One of our generals said 'good morning' to somebody and that was reflected in all the papers as a hideous example of our duplicity."[2]

The feeling naturally arose among members of the Truman administration, fully shared by the American military, that the time when America could influence China, if there ever had been such a time, had long since passed.

But it is necessary to add quickly that as the first year or two of the postwar era marked an effort of the United States to withdraw from China and to pass the Korean problem to the United Nations, the

Republican party in the United States began to show a new life, expecting to win the presidential election of 1948, and part of its tactical maneuvering in foreign policy consisted of stressing the importance of preserving a retreat for the Nationalist Chinese in Formosa, and this in turn put a very special meaning into Korean policy. The truth was that if the Truman administration made any effort to have a stronger policy in Korea, the Republicans would swoop down on the administration and demand more support for the Nationalists in Formosa. Because the administration believed that both places, Korea and Formosa, were indefensible, it had to place a fig leaf (giving Korea to the United Nations) over its Korean awkwardnesses and meanwhile give the impression that Formosa too would be all right. The slightest difficulties in Korea would raise Republican concern that Formosa might be in trouble.

It helped to have General MacArthur presiding over the occupation of Japan, for the Truman administration could claim, with apparent seriousness, that the general was thinking about Korea and Formosa. But there again was a problem, because the more the administration advanced the virtues of MacArthur, the more opportunity it gave an outspoken general—who allowed his supporters to place his name in the Wisconsin primary in 1948 and in nomination at the subsequent GOP national convention—to voice his policy views.

The situation that was awkward politically in the United States was equally awkward for relations between the leader of the Soviet Union, Stalin, and the chairman of the Chinese Communist regime, Mao Tse-tung. Stalin was against Mao's increasing ambition to seize Formosa, as soon as Mao himself triumphed in China proper. Yet the closer Mao came to victory against the Nationalists on the mainland, the less leverage Stalin possessed.

In all these forces and factors, the perhaps determining decision was taken in the United States, and it was a bipartisan decision. This was the resolution of a long debate, beginning at the end of World War II, over the size of the postwar military budget. President Truman wanted it as low as possible, $15 billion or less. He called in General Eisenhower to pacify the squabbling joint chiefs of staff, whose disputes were almost more than Eisenhower could handle. The general's cardiologist believed that Ike suffered a heart attack in 1949, over the strain of trying to hold the military chiefs in some approximation of agreement. At last it was arranged that the military budget for fiscal 1951 (July 1950–June 1951) would be $13 billion or so. The "or so" was a few hundreds of millions, which proved acceptable to all, increasing the budget to $13.5 billion. The then secretary of defense, Johnson, was able to get mileage out of this figure by repeatedly referring to the administration's request as the "Eisenhower budget."[3] Truman, one should add, expected a smaller military budget for fiscal 1952 because of the effect, he announced, of foreign aid.

By this time, the spring of 1950, the American military as well as the Truman administration had made a decision against defending Korea. In July–August 1947 the joint chiefs had advanced their policy to the National Security Council in what became known as NSC-7, a council paper. The result was transferral of the Korean problem to the United Nations, and thereafter the vote establishing the Republic of Korea. As Ambassador John Muccio described this policy, the follow-up would be to "get out of the way in case of trouble."[4] The military policy planners reported to the secretary of defense in 1947 that "from the standpoint of military security, the United States has little strategic interest in maintaining the present troops and bases in Korea."[5] The extension of Soviet control over the entire country would increase that nation's capability "to interfere with United States communications and operations in East China, Manchuria, the Yellow Sea, Sea of Japan and adjacent islands," but the neutralization of such a threat "by air action would be more feasible and less costly than the large-scale ground operations."[6]

The last regular U.S. Army troops, a regimental combat team, left South Korea on June 29, 1949. In June 1950 the only military plan the United States had for Korea was to evacuate the five-hundred-man training force that remained.

2

The precipitating events of the war are not difficult to relate, and one of them was the Sino-Soviet Pact, negotiations for which were in course in Moscow early in January 1950. It seemed like an alarm bell in the night, and yet what could the United States do about it? After Communist China proclaimed victory against the Nationalists by forming a government in Peking in October 1949, it was only natural that the two great communist nations in East Asia, China and the Soviet Union, would express their common purposes in a treaty of alliance.

What statesmen of the West did not know was the almost sullen irritation, the bargaining between the two supposed friends, that marked the weeks of negotiation of the great union of purposes against such malefactors as the United States. Years later the acrimony became known, and it was clear that no love had been lost, that Stalin and Mao were oil and water. The Russian translator at the negotiating sessions remembered that when Stalin walked in everyone seemed to stop breathing, to freeze. "The very room where the talks were held was like a stage where a demonic show was being acted out.... Atmosphere of fear arose."[7] As Mao responded to Soviet points in his coarse Hunan dialect, the translator wondered how these two opponents could ever have anything in common.

Knowing that there were marked differences between the two communist states, but unable to fathom how deep were the personal dislikes, American leaders could do little other than try to make the best of the decision that had been taken by their own military three years before, the decision to get out. In this respect they faced a formidable task, epitomized by the remark of Frederick the Great that diplomacy without armaments was like music without instruments.

The task of making a public statement fell to Secretary of State Acheson, and he did his best. Three of his department advisers, including Rusk, went over to his Georgetown house the night before the secretary was scheduled to give a speech at the National Press Club on January 12 and stayed until 2:00 a.m., trying to find the proper form of words. Something needed to be done, for the Republicans and other critics were claiming that the Truman administration had no Far Eastern policy, nothing to oppose the Sino-Soviet Pact. The decision was taken to draw a perimeter, within which the areas mentioned, including Japan, would if attacked meet with an immediate American military response. The places outside the perimeter would not. Acheson thereupon said what had been decided. It afterward was discovered that he had no text, that he spoke extempore, without notes. This probably made no difference, considering what he had to say.

Nor was this all. In March the secretary of state told the Senate Foreign Relations Committee that there was reason to hope that South Korea could survive and prosper, then added: "This, of course, cannot be guaranteed." The next month, April, an interviewer asked Tom Connally, chairman of the committee, if he thought the United States should abandon South Korea. The answer was what might have been described as unfortunate: "I'm afraid it's going to happen, whether we want it or not." Acheson and Ambassador Muccio quickly issued statements that the American government valued the independence of South Korea.[8]

From the above it might have been possible to say that the damage had been done, but such was not really true, for it had been done in 1947, and behind the military decision of that year, certified by General Eisenhower, had been the belief not merely of the Truman administration's civilian leadership but also of the American military leadership that a military budget of $13 billion to $15 billion was quite all right. Within that belief was, save for the opinion of a few individuals such as General MacArthur, and his opinion only became fairly clear in the months after the Korean War opened, the judgment that Europe was more important than East Asia.

Another interesting point worth making is that Stalin must have known about the decision to give the Korean problem to the United Nations, from the outset, in 1947. The advice of the joint chiefs almost certainly went to the Soviet Union in the form of reports from the Soviet spies in Washington, Donald Maclean and Kim Philby and Guy Burgess.

A momentary uncertainty in the Soviet calculus was the presidential election, with Truman standing for election against the Republican candidate Dewey. Almost everyone, including Bess Truman, thought that the Republicans would win, and one must presume that until that contest's surprise ending the Russians expected not merely a new face in the White House but maybe a stronger policy toward Asian communism. In one sense the Russian dictator could have felt good about a change in U.S. administrations, for President Dewey might have taken a stronger line toward Formosa, undertaking to bolster the Chiang government in its island refuge. That would serve the Soviets, who did not admire Chinese belligerence from Peking, and perhaps take the edge off Chairman Mao's braggadocio. Still, a Republican victory might have carried other awkwardnesses, and in Stalin's mind—and even now, who knows about Stalin's mind?—they might have balanced out.

But then with the Sino-Soviet Pact and the American statement-making and the need to display some assertiveness as befitted a great East Asian communist power, the Soviet government under Stalin found itself confronted with a sudden importuning from the brash leader of North Korea, Kim Il Sung, who began to bombard Stalin with telegrams, forty-eight of them, urging settlement of the Korea problem. In 1949, Kim had sought to encourage guerrilla actions against South Korea, notably around Kaesong. The actions failed; his supporters failed to take a single city. By the end of the year the Syngman Rhee government was beyond question in control in South Korea. It was then that Kim confronted his friend in Moscow with four predictions, all of which proved utterly, disastrously wrong: with Soviet support he could make an attack that would win the war in three days; there would be an uprising by two hundred thousand party members in South Korea; the south contained many guerrillas; the United States would not have time to intervene.

From what we now know, Stalin not merely bought the plan but also gave two pieces of advice to Kim. He suggested the North Korean leader consult with Chairman Mao because he had "a good understanding of Oriental matters."[9] Mao thus was boxed into the decision, for the chairman could not say no to Kim and at the same time, as he indeed was doing, make preparations to invade Formosa that summer. In addition, Stalin advised Kim that Russia was not first among equals in East Asian decisions, thus fastening more responsibility on the hapless Chinese leader. As for Stalin's responsibility, there was none. He made an elegant statement that even if Kim were "kicked in the teeth" by the Americans it would not move the Soviet Union to come to North Korea's aid.[10] All in all the Soviet position was worked out very carefully, in a nice mixture of encouragement and irresponsibility.

The whole thing was a Korean problem. Years later, in moody retirement, Nikita Khrushchev put the situation nicely:

I must stress that the war wasn't Stalin's idea, but Kim Il Sung's. Kim was the initiator. Stalin, of course, didn't try to dissuade him. In my opinion, no real Communist would have tried to dissuade Kim Il Sung from his compelling desire to liberate South Korea from Syngman Rhee and from reactionary American influence. To have done so would have contradicted the Communist view of the world. I don't condemn Stalin for encouraging Kim. On the contrary, I would have made the same decision myself if I had been in his place. Mao Tse-tung also answered affirmatively. He approved Kim Il Sung's suggestion and put forward the opinion that the USA would not intervene since the war would be an internal matter which the Korean people would decide for themselves.[11]

To the leader of the Soviet Union the pluses seemed all on his side. Conquest of South Korea would allow him to widen the buffer on his eastern frontier. He could acquire political, and if necessary military, leverage against Japan. He could test American resolution—if it needed testing, which did not seem to be the case. He could divert American power or, if not that, then attention, from Europe.

With such points in mind the Soviets sent massive amounts of military equipment to the North Koreans, helped them draw up a battle plan, determined the day of attack, thoughtfully did not tell the Chinese about it, and withdrew their military advisers just before the attack itself.

When war broke out there was complete surprise on the American side. Muccio in an oral history said, "We knew of the military material buildup in the north, but it was hard to determine whether this was additional posturing or whether they actually had some action in mind, and if so just when." President Truman said the same thing in his memoirs, that "throughout the spring [of 1950] the Central Intelligence reports said that the North Koreans might at any time decide to change from isolated raids to a full-scale attack," but he himself was sure that war would not come. In fact Truman within days of the opening of the war was thinking of a marked turning point in American foreign relations in which economic policy would prove far more important than military. "It has taken five years to get to this point," he wrote Bess on June 11, 1950. The day before, he had spoken at the Jefferson Memorial in St. Louis, a memorial dedicated to the president who had made the Louisiana Purchase that ensured a great economic future for the country. "The strength of the free world is not to be calculated primarily in military terms," he told his auditors. Economic, political, and moral strength were equally essential, he said. Unconsciously, as we now can see, he was revealing an outlook completely opposite to what the occasion demanded.[12]

Curiously, another interpretation of what happened on June 25, 1950, was possible: many years ago the adviser of the British foreign office on Far Eastern affairs during the 1920s, Sir John Pratt, who incidentally was the half-brother of the screen actor who used the name of Boris Karloff, sent me several articles he wrote in the early 1950s relating that what caused the Korean War was actually an attack by South Korea on North Korea. Sir John and I were corresponding because he had read some of my writings on American East Asian policy under Secretaries of State Charles Evans Hughes, Frank B. Kellogg, and Stimson, and he thought I would be interested twenty and more years later in how policy went wrong. His were well-written articles, and I enjoyed them. There was some plausibility to them, as it was well known within the American government that President Rhee wanted to attack North Korea, and only America's refusal to give his military forces planes and tanks had prevented him from doing exactly that.

But in a long view of history, and even a very short one, there should have been no question as to who had been at fault, and American leaders, civil and military, had not the slightest doubt: it was North Korea, and inside that Trojan horse was the Soviet Union.

3

Last, after looking at the causes of the Korean War, there needs to be some account of the MacArthur dismissal. Once the war was in course there was need to keep American purposes strongly in mind and wind down the war as soon as those purposes were achieved. That General MacArthur did not keep the purposes of his country in mind admits of no debate. When the going became difficult in the early months of the war he advised the national encampment of the Veterans of Foreign Wars, in a statement to be read on August 28, 1950, that Formosa needed defending. At that time it was unclear whether the United States should have or perhaps even could have defended it. President Truman demanded that MacArthur retract the statement, which already was in print in advance copies of a news magazine, and he withdrew it. Six months later, on March 20, 1951, Washington authorities radioed him a proposed presidential statement that looked to a cease-fire and negotiation, and notified him of its imminent release. The general jumped the gun, making the statement himself on March 24, but deleting two paragraphs about consultation with the allies. President Truman said later, "I never was so put out in my life." Then on April 5 came the final act, when the minority leader of the House of Representatives, Joseph W. Martin, read to the House a private letter from the general with the unbending conclusion, "There is no substitute for victory." This was too much, and the president relieved him of his command. He could not "fire" him because MacArthur was a five-star general and hence on the rolls of the U.S. Army for life; Truman merely removed him from his commands.

Admittedly, the president never had admired the general. As early as 1942 the then senator from Missouri wrote his young daughter, "I'm not very fond of MacArthur, if he'd been a real hero he'd have gone down with the ship."[13] As a reserve colonel of artillery in the 1930s, Truman had met Colonel Jonathan M. Wainwright and liked him, and thought it wrong of the senior commander to leave the field, much as Brigadier General Gideon J. Pillow left Fort Donelson in 1862, leaving a subordinate to take the surrender. As World War II progressed, Truman engaged in other remarks about MacArthur, albeit privately, which was assuredly his privilege. Where he erred, doubtless, was in permitting MacArthur to remain in Japan after the war, even though the general had been home only once, for a few weeks in 1937, since he had gone out to the Philippine Islands to train the troops of the Philippine Commonwealth in 1935. Although it was convenient to leave the general in his command, Truman should have brought him home and relieved him. In retirement in 1959 the former president told two friends who were taping his comments that he should have insisted that MacArthur return. He said, "I think, in all probability, I would have relieved him."[14]

On MacArthur's side there was no love lost for the president. When Truman in October 1950 unfortunately succumbed to what probably was a politically inspired meeting with MacArthur at Wake Island, a session of talk that lasted only an hour or two, a small amount of time considering that the president was in the air for hours and hours, MacArthur did not behave well. He flew from Japan with Ambassador Muccio and told the latter of his disgust that he should be interrupted in his important duties by such a session. It is not true that MacArthur's plane sought to wait out the landing of Truman's at Wake, or that MacArthur stood behind the other greeters when the presidential plane landed. It is true that the military men watching the president come down the plane's ramp all saluted him, with the exception of MacArthur, who did not salute.

But whether the two principals enjoyed each other's company was not the question. What was at issue was the strategy of the government of the United States, and on this the president was right and the general wrong. General Matthew B. Ridgway, the hero of the Eighth Army's turnaround, its conversion into a fighting force after the appalling defeat at the Yalu by the Chinese, wrote in an account of the war that at stake were China policy, the proper uses of nuclear power, the brand-new concept of limited war, and the necessary modifications of sovereignty consonant with the obligations laid down in the UN Charter.[15] It is true that MacArthur did not call publicly for a rain of nuclear bombs on China, not to mention the Soviet Union, although he did advocate extending the war to China. In the back of his mind, however, was considerably more. The general's sense of strategy was failing him. In an interview in 1954 given to two reporters whom he warned not to publish his remarks until after his death, he stated that he had desired to drop "between thirty and fifty atomic bombs" on enemy bases.[16] In addition, and the scheme was harebrained, he had the idea of sowing a cobalt belt across the top of North Korea; the belt could be sown by fairly simple means, perhaps by oxcart. Then anyone who walked into it would die, for cobalt had a half-life of sixty-four years.

MacArthur's strategy not merely was wrong, it was impossible. The Truman administration knew only about part of it, the conventional bombing of the Yalu bridges and Chinese staging points. But that was enough to bring MacArthur home. Truman realized that thereafter the very devil would be loose. The general's supporters would see to that. He probably never discovered that former president Hoover called one of the general's former aides, a later vice president of the John Birch Society, and asked him to get in touch with the general and urge him to come home by plane.

MacArthur had planned to come by ship, and changed his mind. The reception was tremendous, comparable only to the enthusiasm for Charles A. Lindbergh when "Lindy" came back from his transatlantic flight of 1927. That the recalled general ended his address to a joint session of Congress with a ridiculous quotation, "Old soldiers never die, they just fade away," made no difference. It was actually an old British Tommy story and meant that old soldiers never died, the young ones did, and the old ones lived on to collect their pensions. This fine point was lost in the hullabaloo.

The hearings that followed the address to Congress and the parades brought out the strategic issue, and gradually everything calmed down. During the hearings Senator Brien McMahon of Connecticut raised a question about Europe and the need for troops. "Well, senator," was the answer, "I am a theater commander and I don't know all of the details that you refer to." McMahon came back to a member of his staff and whispered in his ear, "Now I've got him. I've really got him. He is a theater commander, he doesn't know anything really about what's happening in the rest of the world. The joint chiefs of staff are the only ones who have a knowledge of the whole military responsibility of this government."[17]

The Korean War ran on for more than two additional years after the hearings. It came to its end with the Panmunjom truce of July 1953, in an awkward manner, to put the case mildly. In 2006, fifty-three years after the armistice, American troops still are in South Korea. The line to which General Ridgway's troops had come early in 1951, after they zeroed their artillery in on dense masses of Chinese troops and killed tens of thousands of them, a line that approximated the thirty-eighth parallel with emendations on each side, would hold from 1951 to 1953. During the last year of the war, controversy swirled over what to do about the 130,000 prisoners taken by UN forces, perhaps half of whom did not wish to be repatriated forcibly to North Korea or China. President Truman refused forcible repatriation, which issue prevented an armistice and return of American and South Korean prisoners during his presidency. The North Koreans held 2,500 American prisoners and tens of thousands of South Koreans hostage, many of them taken prisoner in 1950. After South Korean army troops in charge of the UN prisoner camps allowed most of the Korean and Chinese prisoners to escape and remain in South Korea, and after the death of Stalin in March 1953, and despite the threat of the new Eisenhower administration to use nuclear weapons against the North Koreans and their Chinese volunteers (by this time, after the death of Stalin, the Chinese had no more desire to remain in the war and serve Russian policy), the North Korean negotiators prompted by their Chinese friends changed their minds and signed the armistice.

But the United States had redressed a situation that had arisen because of its own inattention and preoccupation, also—let it be added— because of North Korean hotheaded enthusiasm and Russian willingness to take a chance, and similar Chinese hotheadedness and willingness. It was a dangerous situation, which needed to be brought back into order. That, fortunately, is what happened.

Six

Historians on Truman

It is no exaggeration to say that any major public figure, notably a president of the United States, can count on appraisals that run the gamut from fair to unfair, from works of scholarship to works of malevolence. Such has been the case with books about Truman. He was aware that writers would not always treat him well. He was a student—although not always a thorough student—of history, and he enjoyed relating how nineteenth-century New England historians treated President Jefferson for undertaking the Louisiana Purchase. The doubling of American territory by a stroke of Jefferson's pen, when he signed the treaty with Napoleonic France, added a vast frontier region to the country that was bound to overwhelm the Federalist Party and, by New England lights, wreck the very basis for the Union. The New England historians, the twentieth-century president wrote, took it out on Jefferson. As for Truman, he believed the historians would take it out on him because of the program of great measures (Truman Doctrine, Marshall Plan, North Atlantic Treaty) that changed American foreign policy from isolation to participation in world affairs, because of the Korean War, and because of his use of nuclear weapons on Japan. In domestic affairs they would take it out on him because he sought to follow the New Deal of his predecessor with his own Fair Deal. The historians would believe the calumnies of Republican newspaper owners, which had no basis other than their own opinions.

Truman liked to read biographies and admired the Indiana historian Claude G. Bowers, who at long last gave Jefferson his due. He liked Marquis James's books about Jackson. The historians made fun of James, as they did of Bowers, but Truman was a historian, too, and he liked to read about how the "gin-ral" bested his enemies, all for the good of the country. He did not expect the historians immediately to be favorable to his own administration. Time would be necessary for the truth to come out.

Truman did take one measure to avoid the distortions of the historians. This was to authorize a book by his friend Jonathan Daniels, son of Josephus Daniels, who had been secretary of the navy during the Wilson administration. Jonathan Daniels had been a White House assistant during the Franklin Roosevelt administration and for a few days was presidential press secretary in the Truman administration. Truman thought the younger Daniels was too much a scholar for that position, even though he had a connection with his father's newspaper, the *Raleigh News and Observer.* The president replaced him with a high school classmate, Charles G. Ross, a Pulitzer Prize winner with the *St. Louis Post-Dispatch.* Daniels helped write speeches during the 1948 campaign. It may have been with some sense of having hurt Daniels's feelings that Truman allowed Daniels to do an authorized biography. In any event he trusted Daniels and wrote letters of introduction for him to relatives and friends in Independence and Kansas City. Truman himself talked at length with Daniels.

The resultant book (*The Man of Independence,* 1950) was a triumph of the authorized biographer's art. It was always interesting, if overblown in its writing. Daniels, one thinks, pumped up his book's pages to get from there to here. He put in celebrations of the American political past and of the Democratic Party during that past and discussions of the obvious. The book came close to overwriting. Yet he had gone out to Independence and Kansas City and spoken with Truman's contemporaries and even some of his elders. He set down their memories a decade before the archivists of the Truman Library began to do oral histories. By that time, in the 1960s, many of Truman's contemporaries and elders had passed on. Moreover, as Daniels interviewed administration figures, including the president, he obtained a considerable amount of inside information. If separated from the book's celebrations of the Democracy and other explanations, this information is valuable. The book is the only work from the first group of Truman books that amounts to anything, and it is worth reading with care.

Remarking on other first-generation books beyond that of Daniels is hardly worth the effort. A reporter who knew Truman during the Senate years, William P. Helm of the *Kansas City Journal-Post,* had a few interesting things to say, including a story of how in 1941 he persuaded Truman to arrange an investigating committee for the war effort. The committee brought Truman to national attention and made him available for the vice presidential nomination in 1944 (*Harry Truman: A Political Biography,* 1947). A Republican department store owner in Independence, Henry A. Bundschu, published what he described as a biography in 1949, this with the printing facilities of the *Kansas City Star (Harry S. Truman: The Missourian).* Bundschu's account was hardly more than a pamphlet, a few dozen pages. He had known Truman and had stories, and although a Republican he was fair-minded—Truman might have said because he came from Missouri, not New England.

What seems to have been a second wave of scholarship on Truman brought two biographies that appeared in the 1960s and a considerable number of historical monographs on the Truman administration.

The biographies were well done, considering Truman's political eclipse during Eisenhower's presidency and the paucity of available sources on Truman. The library's oral history program was just getting started, and only the general files of the administration were open to researchers. The two authors, Cabell Phillips of the *New York Times* and the freelance writer Alfred Steinberg, must have had little encouragement apart from their own interest. But again, they did well, considering the times and the lack of material. Phillips (*The Truman Presidency,* 1966) possessed thorough knowledge of the presidency, for he had reported it for the *Times.* He was an incisive, well-organized writer. Steinberg (*The Man from Missouri,* 1962) also was a writer, expert at putting together disparate sources, whether interviews with people who had known Truman or memoirs and articles. His was no book to ignore, even though Truman, in annotating his copy, described its author as a liar. As the former president thumbed the book he wrote his impressions in the margins: "Never happened." "Another big lie!" "Another lie." "Not a word of truth in the paragraph." "Lie." "Another lie." "Wrong again." Phillips had irritated Truman by asking to see his private papers. For that matter, so had Steinberg, who accosted Truman when the latter was taking one of his morning walks. To both of these friendly biographers the president said, in effect and possibly in so many words, that he would open his papers when he was good and ready. The books had to be written without their subject's papers or, contrary to the case with Daniels, extended interviews and letters of introduction. With these limitations the books were helpful to readers and informative. They came as close as the authors could get.

The monographs on Truman that appeared in this second wave were drawn from similar sources—the library's general files together with whatever collections of private papers were open, most of them in the library. The books were usually by academic scholars who used newspapers and the *Congressional Record* and articles in journals that themselves suffered from the same limitations as the biographies.[1]

A third grouping of the Truman literature consisted of the books that came out in the 1970s. Here there were two more biographies. The one by Margaret Truman was by and large a worthwhile volume (*Harry S. Truman,* 1973). Written with the assistance of Thomas Fleming, it contained novelties, for the president's daughter was as forthright as her father and had been in a position to know a great deal. It is an affectionate book and defensive, and Margaret Truman made no effort to hide her partisanship. She showed her father as an enormously hardworking chief executive, doing his best for the country over not merely the years of the presidency but also the twenty years of county and Senate officeholding that preceded them.

The other biography that came out at this time was *Plain Speaking: An Oral Biography of Harry S. Truman* (1973) by the newspaperman and writer Merle Miller. Based on tapings of the president in 1960–

1961 in preparation for a television series that failed to attract network sponsorship, the book entranced reviewers and readers and many scholars. The latter have quoted from its pages down to the present time. Margaret Truman's book sold well, into the hundreds of thousands of copies. Miller's book sold better: in two years 500,000 hardcover copies and 1.25 million paperbacks. Margaret Truman did not like Miller's book at all. To a Kansas City reporter she said that her father undoubtedly said the things in the book but that Miller, who had been a writer for the proposed television series, had no right to use the tapes. She was not certain about who owned the tapes and presumed that their ownership was subject to common-law copyright, the same as letters, by which the writer of a letter possessed copyright even though the recipient or someone else held the letter.

The Miller book deserves attention because so many copies are in the hands of readers who accept it as containing the president's very words. Only recently has it been possible to verify its contents. Suffice it to say that, although the book was distributed by a reputable New York firm, Putnam, and has had a long life and is still in print, it was a gross literary fraud. Miller took unpardonable liberties with the president's words on tape. Actually, Miller had little to do with the tapings. Two friends of the president, the radio reporter William Hillman and a public relations man and former presidential assistant, David M. Noyes, asked the questions, with Miller occasionally chiming in. Somehow the tapes came into Miller's possession, and he used them for all they were worth and a good deal more. Years after bringing out his book, and after a reported public row with Margaret Truman, he gave the tapes to the Lyndon B. Johnson Library in Austin, Texas. Austin was a remote locality, and the self-designated oral biographer ensured the tapes' remoteness by closing them. He died in 1986, and in 1993 officials of the Johnson and Truman libraries realized that the tapes had not belonged to Miller in the first place and opened them. The opening was heralded by a press release, and the present writer drove out from Bloomington, Indiana, to Independence for the occasion. No one else turned up except a National Park Service researcher who spent a half hour, found nothing about the Ethel and Nellie Noland house at 216 North Delaware, across the street from the Truman house at 219 North Delaware, and went away. After listening to the tapes and attempting to transcribe them using a primitive recorder purchased at a local discount store, I gave up and ordered copies and had them transcribed. Miller's modus operandi stood revealed. He changed Truman's words in countless ways, sometimes improving the literary effect. Adding or subtracting words, he thoughtfully added his own opinions. He inserted his favorite cuss words, damning Truman for two generations as a foul-mouthed old man. He cutely claimed the president to have been a drinker, to have imbibed during the taping sessions by stepping out for (he presumed—he had no way of knowing) "small libations." He said he accompanied the president to a Howard Johnson restaurant near the library—a preposterous claim, for Truman would have been overwhelmed with autograph seekers. There, in the restaurant, Miller and Truman drank more libations. Worst of all, Miller made up many pages in his book, inventing whole chapters. The material on President Eisenhower, which composes much of the book, is almost entirely invention. Notably the tapes say nothing about the story that most attracted readers to the book. This was the detailing of an alleged intervention by General Marshall (all this is in Truman's words) against Eisenhower, who during the war (according to Miller) desired a divorce from his wife so he could marry his pretty driver and receptionist, Kay Summersby. It is possible that Miller obtained such gossip from Truman's military aide, Major General Harry H. Vaughan, who after the book came out vouched for the story.

The Truman monographs of the 1970s, books that were various and sundry in their subjects, often reflected the passions of the Vietnam War, which had come to a crisis in 1968 and then wound down until the collapse of South Vietnam. The outstanding book of the decade was not about Vietnam but about American liberalism, which, as its author, Alonzo L. Hamby, related, was in trouble during the Truman years.[2]

Another reason the monographs of the 1970s were not going to stand over the years was that the major (not in quantity, but in quality) holdings of the Truman Library did not open until the late 1970s and early 1980s. These were, first of all, the private papers of the president, 339 Hollinger boxes, each five inches wide and holding file folders of letters and memos and other such things. The opening of this treasure trove began in 1977 and was almost entirely complete by 1980. It was followed by a second trove, the most remarkable set of private papers in the history of the presidency: 1,268 letters from Truman to Bess Wallace and, after their marriage in 1919, Bess W. Truman. All but one were in the president's hand. They were written between 1910 and 1959. The letters were found in the Truman house a few blocks from the library and opened in 1983, a year after Bess's death. They were everywhere in the house—in boxes downstairs, in bureau drawers, under sofa cushions. Those in the attic were stored amid confusions that would make any historian shudder. The attic was open to animals and birds, and a raccoon got in and discovered jars of jellies or other preserves, clawed open the lids, and enjoyed himself, after which he feasted on the attic's pigeons. All over the attic were clutches of pigeon feathers and jam. But the letters were all saved and brought down to the library, except for some dozens, maybe hundreds, that Bess had burned. Her daughter once described this in a book (*Souvenir: Margaret Truman's Own Story,* 1956). According to Margaret Truman, her father came into the living room where Bess was burning letters in the fireplace. "But think of history!" said the president. "I *have,*" was the response.

Another treasure of the library that became available at the same time as the private papers and Dear Bess letters was the diary of Truman's assistant press secretary, Eben A. Ayers. The diary set down in enormous detail—half a million words—what went on in the executive offices each day and especially what happened in the president's office, which was a few feet from Ayers's office.

Beginning in the 1980s, because of the wonderful new material, a new group of books has appeared. At long last, two generations after Truman's presidency and three decades and more since his death in 1972, the literature is beginning to take the measure of the man and his times. Robert J. Donovan in 1977 and 1982 published remarkable books on each of the Truman terms *(Conflict and Crisis* and *Tumultuous Years).* Donald R. McCoy published a volume on the presidency (*The Presidency of Harry S. Truman,* 1984). Richard Lawrence Miller took Truman to the White House in *Truman: The Rise to Power* (1986), based on careful work in the library. William E. Pemberton, in *Harry S. Truman: Fair Dealer and Cold Warrior* (1989), revived the contentions of the revisionists, using the new material. Monte M. Poen published the Truman "mad

letters," a marvelous collection of missives in which the president cus-
tomarily began on a cool note and gradually lost his temper, forcing
him or his secretary, Rose Conway, to file the result (*Strictly Personal and
Confidential,* 1982). Poen published another admirable collection on a
variety of subjects (*Letters Home,* 1984). Andrew J. Dunar reexamined
the Truman scandals in a measured, fair way (*The Truman Scandals
and the Politics of Morality,* 1984). Ken Hechler, a former White House
assistant, brought out his authoritative *Working with Truman* (1982).

Three large biographies have been published. Casting about in 1982
for a subject that would hold his attention and that of readers, David
McCullough considered Pablo Picasso. When that subject wore out more
quickly than he thought possible, he turned to Truman (*Truman,* 1992).
In time for the presidential campaign of that year, the book's stories
about its subject, its drawing of Truman as a son of the Middle Border,
and its appreciation of the American past at a time when nostalgia was
in short supply made it irresistible to book buyers. The present writer
published *Harry S. Truman: A Life* in 1994, a volume quite different
from McCullough's in that it is not a "life and times" and thereby is half
as long. Reviewers have said it is more critical of its subject. Alonzo
Hamby in 1995 brought out another life and times *(Man of the People).*
It does not celebrate the Middle Border, even though Hamby is a native
of Humansville (population 1,084), one of those wonderful Missouri
farm villages with piquant names, such as Peculiar. Hamby's book offers
a psychological view of its subject. He presents him as an overachiever
who worked harder than other individuals because he was unsure of
himself.

In the midst of the appearance of the biographies occurred the confusion in Washington over the proposed exhibit at the Air and Space
Museum that would consider the controversial issue of the dropping of
nuclear bombs in 1945 and feature the *Enola Gay,* the B-29 bomber
that delivered the Hiroshima atomic bomb. The museum's curators had
prepared a text to accompany the items on exhibit that seemed to service historians and veterans to be too evenhanded in assessing responsibility for the war and to criticize use of the bomb. Revisions were made,
and they too did not please the service historians and veterans. Historians generally entered the fray, with perhaps a dozen books in 1995,

some justifying use of the bomb, others criticizing. The criticism looked in the direction of the reputation of the president. On more than one occasion Truman had justified what he had done. In 1959 he told an enormous twelve-hundred-student "class" at Columbia University that the bomb was just like an ordinary artillery weapon, that the Japanese deserved it, that he lost no sleep over the decision, and if necessary he would make the same decision.

Has the evaluation of Truman and his place in history come to rest? Here we must distinguish between the views of the American public, which bought McCullough's book, and those of historians, who may not have bought it. The American public long ago went over to Truman's side, a process that began in the early 1970s with the abject end of the Nixon administration. By that time busloads of tourists were filling the semicircular road outside the library, and inside citizens were fighting for souvenirs. *Time* magazine described the scene as "Trumania."

The three recent biographers agree with the public view. In McCullough's evaluation and my own and Hamby's, no more sorting of Truman's qualities needs to be done. In spite of my criticisms of Truman's public career, and Hamby's sensitivity to Truman's personal insecurities, all of us place him high among holders of his office. His foreign policy by and large turned out right. Everything coming from the archives of the former Soviet Union has backed Truman up, including the recent discovery that Stalin was responsible for starting the Korean War.[3] As for Truman's domestic proposals, the country in the years after his presidency accepted all of them, save his proposal for health care—about which he may have been prescient (for what was the country coming to, Truman once asked himself, when it was possible for a working man to pay as much as twenty-five dollars a day for a hospital bed?).

From this positive judgment the historians generally have held back. They have not yet come around to Truman, certainly not to Trumania. For them the new Truman books, the biographies and the others using the new material, have not made much of a difference. Perhaps they think that David McCullough is only another Claude Bowers or Marquis James. For myself and Hamby, they may believe that we have spent too much time in the library and have been overwhelmed by Truman's presence there. His grave is in the library courtyard, outside the windows of the search room. Taken as a group the historians are not enthusiastic about Truman and his works.[4] This is the case even though the polls of historians and other experts in the ranking of presidents have shown Truman as eighth or ninth in what is becoming a large group. In evaluating Truman the historians by and large find themselves uncertain. They need more time before they come around to the right point of view.

Chapter One. Revisionism

Originally published in Richard S. Kirkendall, ed., *The Truman Period as a Research Field: A Reappraisal, 1972,* 11–46.

1. John L. Snell, "The Cold War: Four Contemporary Appraisals."

2. Ronald Steel, *Imperialists and Other Heroes: A Chronicle of the American Empire,* 6–7.

3. Walter LaFeber's *The New Empire: An Interpretation of American Expansion, 1860–1898,* winner of the Beveridge Prize of the American Historical Association, was published by Cornell University Press in 1963.

4. Lloyd C. Gardner, *Economic Aspects of New Deal Diplomacy,* was published by the University of Wisconsin Press in 1964.

5. Irwin Unger, "The New Left and American History: Some Recent Trends in United States Historiography," 1248.

6. Walter LaFeber, ed., *Origins of the Cold War, 1941–1947: Documents and Problems,* 3; Stephen E. Ambrose, "The Failure of a Policy Rooted in Fear."

7. Carl Degler, review of *The Roots of the Modern American Empire* by William A. Williams, in *American Historical Review* 75 (1969–1970): 1780–82.

8. John L. Gaddis, "Domestic Influences on American Policy toward the Soviet Union, 1941–1947." I am much indebted to Gaddis for a copy of this perceptive paper.

9. Ibid.; see also Charles S. Maier, "Revisionism and the Interpretation of Cold War Origins."

10. Arthur M. Schlesinger Jr., "The Velocity of History," *Newsweek,* July 6, 1970.

11. Adam Ulam, "On Modern History: Re-reading the Cold War," *Interplay Magazine* 2 (March 1968): 51–53, reprinted in part in Thomas G. Paterson, ed., *The Origins of the Cold War.*

12. Barton J. Bernstein, "Walter Lippmann and the Early Cold War," in Thomas G. Paterson, ed., *Cold War Critics: Alternatives to American Foreign Policy in the Truman Years,* 32, 46, 56.

13. Lloyd C. Gardner, *Architects of Illusion: Men and Ideas in American Foreign Policy, 1941–1949,* 6.

14. Beatrice Farnsworth, *William C. Bullitt and the Soviet Union.*

15. John Gimbel, *The American Occupation of Germany: Politics and the Military, 1945–1949.* The quotation appears in his article "Cold War: German Front."

16. Walter LaFeber, *America, Russia, and the Cold War,* 20. LaFeber's documentary volume, *Origins of the Cold War, 1941–1947,* printed the Sloan letter as Document 34 (pp. 129–31); Document 33 is the Potsdam agreement on Germany, and Document 35 is Secretary of State James F. Byrnes's Stuttgart speech of September 6, 1946.

17. David Donald, "Radical Historians on the Move."

18. The revisionists had a field day with their scholarship because historians failed to examine their footnotes other than to be impressed with the variety and quantity. A historian went behind those notes, back to the sources, and checked the contexts of quotations, watching closely for the use of ellipsis points. It turned out that the footnotes were a mosaic of misrepresentation. See Robert J. Maddox, "Cold War Revisionism: Abusing History." This article was introduced by Oscar Handlin, the distinguished Harvard historian, who was in the fore of unbelievers in revisionism. Maddox's *The New Left and the Origins of the Cold War* enlarged on the above theme with chapters on Williams, D. F. Fleming, Horowitz, Alperovitz, Kolko, Diane Shaver Clemens, and Gardner. With its publication in June 1973 a furious debate opened between revisionists and their opponents, one perceptive individual describing the confrontation as "the historians' Watergate." As for Tansill's use of materials, I was once shown confidentially a most painstaking analysis of the footnotes to his *Back Door to War,* the volume he and his supporters claimed was based on the Department of State archives. It certainly was—whenever Tansill was proving a commonplace. When he came to crucial points, his State Department documentation thinned down to nothing. But he found the unpublished department records helpful in other ways; his many impressive citations to newspapers indicated that he used the department's press surveys without attribution, an odd procedure for a scholar who maintained that one could not trust the Department of State.

19. Baruch had threatened to leave the reservation during debate over the Truman Doctrine, largely because the president had the temerity to recommend Greek-Turkish aid without consulting Baruch. The president's advisers had difficulty in bringing him around, for Truman flatly refused to court the old man. The president's counsel, Clark Clifford, told Lilienthal, who put the

remark in his diary (entry of March 23, 1947), that the president said, "I'm just not going to do it. I'm not going to spend hours and hours on that old goat, come what may. If you take his advice, then you have him on your hands for hours and hours, and it is his policy. I'm not going to do it" (*The Journals of David E. Lilienthal*, 2:163–64). The president said there was a decision to make and it was going to be made. Secretary of the Navy James V. Forrestal gave a dinner for Baruch at which Secretary of War Robert P. Patterson and Secretary of Commerce W. Averell Harriman were guests; beforehand, Forrestal called up Lewis Strauss, who also was to attend, and told him that the purpose of the meeting was "to grease the old boy." About this time Lilienthal was moving carefully with Baruch for another reason, and noted, "They really work at it, too. Everyone does. Everyone, apparently, but the President, who says he just won't." For another piece of Baruchiana, see my *George C. Marshall,* 223.

20. Paterson in his edited volume, *Cold War Critics,* brought together essays on these men, together with chapters on Robert A. Taft, black critics of colonialism and the cold war, I. F. Stone and the Korean War, and the threat to civil liberties.

21. Gar Alperovitz, *Cold War Essays,* 92. See also Gardner, *Architects of Illusion,* 354; LaFeber, ed., *Origins of the Cold War,* 171.

22. John L. Gaddis, *The United States and the Origins of the Cold War, 1941–1947,* vii.

23. Dexter Perkins, in *AHA Newsletter,* May 1971.

24. A conference of researchers and archivists, sponsored by the General Services Administration and held at the National Archives in the summer of 1969, introduced many scholars to the complexities of the national records, and details appeared in successive issues of *Prologue,* the Archives journal.

25. Athan G. Theoharis, *The Yalta Myths: An Issue in U.S. Politics, 1945–1955* and *Seeds of Repression: Harry S. Truman and the Origins of McCarthyism.*

26. Thomas G. Paterson and Les Adler, "Red Fascism: The Merger of Nazi Germany and Soviet Russia in the American Image of Totalitarianism, 1930's-1950's." The essay produced an unprecedented flow of letters to the editor, to which the authors responded with as much heat and sarcasm as the critics bestowed. See *American Historical Review* 75 (1969–1970): 2155–64; 76 (1970–1971): 575–80, 856–58.

27. Alonzo Hamby, "The Liberals, Truman, and FDR as Symbol and Myth," 865.

28. "He had never been spoken to like that before, exclaimed Molotov. But knowing who his boss was, one must assume that the Soviet statesman was exaggerating" (Adam B. Ulam, *The Rivals: America and Russia since World War II,* 64).

29. Arthur M. Schlesinger Jr., "Origins of the Cold War."

30. William M. Franklin, "Zonal Boundaries and Access to Berlin"; David Herschler, "Retreat in Germany: The Decision to Withdraw Anglo-American Forces from the Soviet Occupational Zone, 1945."

31. Herbert Feis, *From Trust to Terror: The Onset of the Cold War, 1945–1950,* 17–19.

32. Ibid.; also Richard L. Walker and George Curry, *Edward R. Stettinius, Jr., and James F. Byrnes.* Curry based his account on close personal consultation with Byrnes and had access to the Byrnes papers. He assisted the secretary in the research and writing of his autobiography.

33. Schlesinger, in "Origins of the Cold War," 24n, published an account of a conversation between Anna Rosenberg Hoffman and FDR, March 24, 1945, the last day Roosevelt spent in Washington. After luncheon the president was handed a cable, read it, and became angry. He banged his fists on the arms of his wheelchair and said, "Averell is right; we can't do business with Stalin. He has broken every one of the promises he made at Yalta."

34. "Frère Jacques" Duclos, the comintern official in charge of the Western communist parties, in the April 1945 issue of *Cahiers du Communisme* launched an attack on the American communist party, condemning Earl Browder's revisionism. Schlesinger, in "Origins of the Cold War," says that he could not have planned and written this piece much later than the Yalta Conference, therefore it showed Stalin turning against the West well before the incidents the revisionists cited to demonstrate American responsibility for the cold war. The revisionists stressed the unimportance of the letter or Schlesinger's misinterpretation of it.

35. Melvin Croan, "Origins of the Post-War Crisis—a Discussion," excerpted in Paterson, ed., *Origins of the Cold War,* 112.

36. Feis, *From Trust to Terror,* 26.

37. Gar Alperovitz, *Cold War Essays,* 4.

38. Adam Ulam, "On Modern History: Re-reading the Cold War," excerpted in Paterson, ed., *Origins of the Cold War,* 115.

39. Alperovitz, *Cold War Essays,* 5. The psychology is on 71: "Thus it appears that the natural military assumption that the bomb would be used became intermeshed with diplomatic strategy in a way so subtle it was probably not completely understood by the participants themselves."

40. Alperovitz needed to show that there was no military justification for the bomb. This was his key piece of evidence, because it would mean that President Truman had ulterior reasons for using atomic weapons. In *Atomic Diplomacy: Hiroshima and Potsdam, the Use of the Atomic Bomb and the American Confrontation with Soviet Power,* 237–38, Alperovitz wrote: "*Before the atomic bomb was dropped each of the Joint Chiefs of Staff advised that it was highly likely that Japan could be forced to surrender 'unconditionally,' without use of the bomb and without an invasion* [Alperovitz's italics]. Indeed, this characterization of the position taken by the senior military advisers is a conservative one. General Marshall's June 18 appraisal was the most cautiously phrased advice offered by any of the Joint Chiefs: 'The impact of Russian entry on the already hopeless Japanese may well be the decisive action levering them into capitulation. . . . '" The ellipsis points at the end of this quotation were Alperovitz's, after which he passed to the opinion of Admiral Leahy. For the quotation from Marshall, Alperovitz cited Potsdam documents in *Foreign Relations,* but careful reading of *Foreign Relations of the United States: The Conference of*

Berlin, 1945, 1:905, the same page used by Alperovitz, makes it clear that Marshall anticipated the necessity of American troops landing on Kyushu, an operation then being planned for November 1, and that it might even be necessary to land troops on Honshu, the island containing Tokyo, which latter landing eventually was scheduled for March 1, 1946. Following is a properly full quotation of Marshall's opinion (in the document the general was reading, the designation "Japan" meant the Honshu landing): "There is reason to believe that the first 30 days in Kyushu should not exceed the price we have paid for Luzon. It is a grim fact that there is not an easy, bloodless way to victory in war and it is the thankless task of the leaders to maintain their firm outward front which holds the resolution of their subordinates. Any irresolution in the leaders may result in costly weakening and indecision in the subordinates.... [Ellipsis in original.] An important point about Russian participation in the war is that the impact of Russian entry on the already hopeless Japanese may well be the decisive action levering them into capitulation *at that time or shortly thereafter if we land in Japan.*" Alperovitz omitted these final, italicized words and failed to print the preceding two sentences, lifting his quotation completely out of context. I am indebted to Garry Clifford of the University of Connecticut, who in 1968–1969 devoted part of a seminar at the University of Tennessee to the Alperovitz book, for calling attention to this use of quotation.

41. Stimson diary, Yale University. I am indebted to Lisle A. Rose for this quotation.

42. Diary of Chancellor of the Exchequer Hugh Dalton, in Feis, *From Trust to Terror,* 98.

43. Lisle A. Rose, *After Yalta,* 124.

44. Ibid., 140.

45. Schlesinger, "Origins of the Cold War," 45.

46. George C. Herring, "Lend-Lease to Russia and the Origins of the Cold War, 1944–1945."

47. Soviet unwillingness in 1945 to follow up the Molotov proposal produced a difficult situation for the Americans. Should the United States have taken the initiative?

48. Thomas G. Paterson, "The Abortive American Loan to Russia and the Origins of the Cold War, 1943–1946," 77.

49. Ibid., 70–71.

50. Dalton diary, quoted in Ferrell, *George C. Marshall,* 117.

51. Ulam, *The Rivals,* 119.

52. *Foreign Relations of the United States, 1946,* vol. VII, *The Near East and Africa,* 348–49.

53. LaFeber, *America, Russia, and the Cold War,* 30.

54. "The epoch of isolation and occasional intervention is ended. It is being replaced by an epoch of American responsibility." *New York Times,* March 12, 1947.

55. Barnet, *Intervention and Revolution: America's Confrontation with Insurgent Movements around the World,* 97–131.

56. Gardner, *Architects of Illusion*, 224; James F. Byrnes, *Speaking Frankly*, 302.

57. Theoharis, *Seeds of Repression;* Richard M. Freeland, *The Truman Doctrine and the Origins of McCarthyism: Foreign Policy, Domestic Politics, and Internal Security, 1946–1948.* Review by Christopher Lehmann-Haupt, *New York Times Book Review*, January 21, 1972.

58. Steel, *Imperialists and Other Heroes,* 23. Steel entitled his chapter on Acheson, a reprinted review of *Present at the Creation*, "Commissar of the Cold War."

59. William V. Shannon, *New York Times*, January 16, 1972.

60. Paterson, ed., *Cold War Critics*, 132.

61. Paterson suggested use of the Economic Commission for Europe in his "The Quest for Peace and Prosperity: International Trade, Communism, and the Marshall Plan," in Barton J. Bernstein, ed., *Politics and Policies of the Truman Administration*, 100.

62. Klaus Epstein, "The German Problem, 1945–1950." See U.S. Senate, Committee on Foreign Relations, *Documents on Germany, 1944–1970*, especially 195ff., for the 1952 proposal.

63. Lloyd C. Gardner, "America and the German 'Problem,' 1945–1949," in Bernstein, ed., *Politics and Policies*, 113–48; John Gimbel, "Cold War: German Front." Clay was concerned about communism born of desperation. As for fear of the virus of socialism, an ideological concern, that was a dubious point.

Chapter Two. The Bomb — the View from Washington

Originally a paper given at the annual meeting of the Society for Military History, Pennsylvania State University, State College, Pennsylvania, April 16, 1999.

1. Barton J. Bernstein, "A Postwar Myth: 500,000 Lives Saved."

2. The article by Asada appeared in 1998. The next year saw publication of Richard B. Frank, *Downfall: The End of the Imperial Japanese Empire,* which supported Asada. A longtime student of Japanese-American relations, Asada is bilingual. Frank does not read Japanese but engaged an able translator. Tsuyoshi Hasegawa, *Racing the Enemy: Stalin, Truman, and the Surrender of Japan,* followed in 2005. Asada had taken the position that surrender occurred because of the shock of the bomb and that the bomb hence was necessary. Hasegawa believed that surrender came not merely because of the bomb but also because of the shock of Russian entry. The bomb hence might not have been necessary. The literature in English regarding the effect of Soviet entry upon surrender is slight. Japanese sources offer little on the subject. Asada concluded that the decision to surrender was taken before Russian entry; Hasegawa may have speculated in this regard. The Hasegawa book seems an unfortunate contribution in another way, for it places the responsibility for use of nuclear weapons evenly on Japan, Russia, and the United States. The author ignores the behavior of the Japanese Army in its conquests beginning with the Sino-Japanese

War in 1937, in which the death toll of prisoners and civilians alike ran into the millions; the United Nations figure is seventeen million, the Chinese thirty. For the Americans this meant the Bataan death march, among many other bestialities. In 1945, with the imminence of the attack on Kyushu, the vice minister of war sent out an order that when the first American landed on one of the home islands there should be the immediate execution, by any means, of all Allied prisoners held within the empire, whose numbers were estimated at one hundred thousand.

3. The present essay was given at a conference session in which all the participants maintained that the bomb was necessary to surrender.

4. On June 18, General Marshall told the president that the Japanese Army had 350,000 men on Kyushu. At the beginning of August the figure was 600,000. At the end of the war the confirmed figure was 900,000.

5. See Robert H. Ferrell, *The Dying President: Franklin D. Roosevelt, 1944–1945*, 73–74.

6. Robert H. Ferrell, ed., *FDR's Quiet Confidant: The Autobiography of Frank C. Walker*, 150.

7. A colleague in the department of history at Indiana University, John E. Wilz, read from a textbook to a class for an hour, completing five pages, when it was possible to read, by oneself, twenty to twenty-five pages.

8. Box 43, White House confidential file, Truman papers, Truman Library. According to archivist Dennis E. Bilger, Truman's private secretary, Rose Conway, used this file, of less than fifty Hollinger boxes, for wartime material that came from the State Department, with addition of Truman's requests and replies.

9. The navy was contending that an invasion was unnecessary and that Japan could be blockaded into surrender.

10. D. M. Giangreco and Kathryn Moore, "Half a Million Purple Hearts."

Chapter Three. Diplomacy without Armaments

Originally published in Scott L. Bills and E. Timothy Smith, eds., *The Romance of History: Essays in Honor of Lawrence S. Kaplan*, 35–49. Reprinted with permission of Kent State University Press.

1. Omar N. Bradley and Clay Blair, *A General's Life: An Autobiography*, 474.

2. Ibid.

3. Tang Tsou, "Civil Strife and Armed Intervention: Marshall's China Policy," 89–90.

4. David Alan Rosenberg, "U.S. Nuclear Stockpile 1945 to 1950," 27–29.

5. Robert H. Ferrell, ed., *Truman in the White House: The Diary of Eben A. Ayers*, 161, entry of October 14, 1945; Ferrell, ed., "A Visit to the White House, 1947: The Diary of Vic H. Housholder," 329; Gregg Herken, *The Winning Weapon: The Atomic Bomb in the Cold War, 1945–1950*, 196–97.

6. Samuel R. Williamson Jr. and Steven L. Rearden, *The Origins of U.S. Nuclear Strategy, 1945–1953*, 125. The purpose of the Soviets' investigation of

radar jamming could also have been to confuse SAC's targeting, which was based on synthetic radar images. Rearden to the author, September 27, 1993.

7. Harry R. Borowski, *A Hollow Threat: Strategic Air Power and Containment before Korea.*

8. Verne W. Newton, *The Cambridge Spies: The Untold Story of Maclean, Philby, and Burgess in America.*

Chapter Four. NATO

Originally published in Lawrence S. Kaplan, ed., *American Historians and the Atlantic Alliance,* 11–32. Reprinted with permission of Kent State University Press.

1. Walt W. Rostow, *The Stages of Economic Growth: A Non-Communist Manifesto,* chaps. 2–4.

2. H. R. Trevor-Roper, "The Lost Moments of History."

3. "Whatever their views, most cold-war historians have neglected an important topic: the military capability of the major powers. Most would agree that military strength largely determines how vigorously or extensively a nation may pursue foreign policy objectives, but few historians have paid serious attention to such capabilities in their studies.... As a result, scholars have made uncritical assumptions about military capability, particularly that of the United States" (Harry R. Borowski, *A Hollow Threat: Strategic Air Power and Containment before Korea,* 3).

4. Melvyn P. Leffler, "The American Conception of National Security and the Beginnings of the Cold War, 1945–1948."

5. Richard A. Best Jr., *"Co-operation with Like-Minded Peoples": British Influences on American Security Policy, 1943–1949,* 181.

6. Ibid., 185–86.

7. Theodore Achilles, oral history by Richard D. McKinzie, November 13, 18, 1972, 25, Truman Library; André Beaufre, *NATO and Europe,* 27.

8. Borowski, *Hollow Threat,* 116–17.

9. Ibid., 100–101.

10. David Alan Rosenberg, "American Atomic Strategy and the Hydrogen Bomb Decision," 64, 68–69; Thomas H. Etzold and John L. Gaddis, eds., *Containment: Documents on American Policy and Strategy, 1945–1950,* 318.

11. David E. Lilienthal, *The Journals of David E. Lilienthal,* 2:464.

12. Robert H. Ferrell, ed., *The Eisenhower Diaries,* 157.

13. Rosenberg, "U.S. Nuclear Stockpile"; Steven L. Rearden, *History of the Office of the Secretary of Defense,* 1:439. Rosenberg offers no figures for mid-1949 but says there were at least 292 bombs by mid-1950 and four hundred by January 1, 1951; Rearden has no figures beyond mid-1948. President Truman seems to have been fairly well versed on the size of the stockpile. Rosenberg in "American Atomic Strategy and the Hydrogen Bomb Decision," 66, relates

that the president did not even know the stockpile's size until his first briefing by Lilienthal on April 3, 1947, when he appeared to be shocked by the figure Lilienthal gave him (Lilienthal, *Journals,* 2:165–66). According to Rosenberg, Lilienthal told the president there were seven complete weapons; more nuclear cores were available, but there was a shortage of polonium initiators. But someone was giving figures to the president, and in his later article on the stockpile Rosenberg presumes it was General Eisenhower, army chief of staff in 1945–1948 (the Manhattan Project was under army control in 1945–1946). According to Eben A. Ayers, assistant White House press secretary, who attended Truman's morning conferences, on October 14, 1946, Truman said he "did not believe that there were over a half dozen" bombs in the stockpile (Ferrell, ed., *Truman in the White House,* 161). This figure would have been about right, considering that nine bombs were ready by June 30, and the two Bikini tests followed. Moreover, on February 7–8, 1947, also before Lilienthal briefed Truman, the president entertained his World War I first lieutenant in Battery D, 129th Field Artillery Regiment, Vic Housholder, who stayed overnight in the White House, and told him there were fourteen atomic bombs (Ferrell, ed., "A Visit to the White House, 1947," 329). The Rosenberg-Rearden figure for June 30, 1947, is thirteen, and because of the problem with polonium initiators the figure Truman told Housholder must have been momentarily correct.

14. Borowski, *Hollow Threat,* 83.

15. Ibid., 167.

16. President Truman and foreign ministers meeting, April 3, 1949, in Lawrence S. Kaplan, *The United States and NATO: The Formative Years,* 6.

17. The quotation continues: ". . . and the vast problem of subduing a sprawling empire stretching from Kamchatka to the Skaggerak with this weapon, to say nothing of the problem of using it against our occupied Western European allies. In any case, a Soviet attack today, while we could eventually defeat it, would involve an operation of incalculable magnitude in which, even if eventual victory is sure, the consequences to the U.S., and particularly to Western Europe, might well be disastrous" (ibid.).

18. Robert L. Dennison, oral history by Jerry N. Hess, September 10, 1971, 22, Truman Library.

19. Interview in *New York Times Book Review,* October 12, 1969.

20. John L. Gaddis critiqued Leffler's article, and in reply the author stressed his conclusions. "Accordingly, I find Professor Gaddis's emphasis on the Soviet military threat in Eurasia very misleading. Soviet military capabilities did not constitute 'a threat of the first order,' because neither American officials nor European statesmen expected Soviet military aggression" (Leffler, "The American Conception of National Security," 396). As for the manner in which American officials, military and civil, created their own problem: "Professor Gaddis wrote in *Strategies of Containment* that the Truman administration 'lost sight of the objective that strength was supposed to serve: ending the Cold War.' What Gaddis failed to recognize is that strength was not designed to end the

Cold War; strength was designed to achieve the national security objectives I describe in my essay, regardless of the impact on the Cold War or on the Soviet Union. And the result of this may have been to discourage Soviet leaders from defining their opportunities in terms of a cooperative as well as a competitive relationship with the United States" (ibid., 398–99).

21. Ibid., 359–60; Truman's note of March 5 is in "Cabinet—meetings, 1946–50," President's Secretary's Files, box 154, Truman Library; for the Truman testimony of September 13, 1948, see Robert H. Ferrell, *George C. Marshall*, 246–47; of August 31, 1949, Ayers diary of that date, in Ferrell, ed., *Truman in the White House*, 326.

22. Alan Bullock, *Ernest Bevin: Foreign Secretary, 1945–1951*, 614–682; Dean Acheson, *Sketches from Life of Men I Have Known*, 1; Ayers diary, January 10, 22, March 21, 1949, in Ferrell, ed., *Truman in the White House*, 289, 291, 299–300; John D. Hickerson, oral history by Richard D. McKinzie, 53–54, Truman Library.

23. John R. Colville, "The Personality of Sir Winston Churchill," address at Westminster College, Fulton, Missouri, March 24, 1985, in R. Crosby Kemper III, ed., *Winston Churchill: Resolution, Defiance, Magnanimity, Good Will*, 108–25.

24. Lewis W. Douglas to Lovett, April 12, 1948, in *Foreign Relations of the United States, 1948*, vol. III, *Western Europe*, 90. When the Soviets obtained the atomic bomb, Churchill said, war was a certainty.

25. Achilles oral history, in Lawrence S. Kaplan and Sidney R. Snyder, eds., *"Fingerprints on History": The NATO Memoirs of Theodore C. Achilles*, 8–9, 12, 26; Kaplan, *United States and NATO*, 58. As for the punch, Achilles explained that the Metropolitan Club in Washington always held open house on Christmas Eve and New Year's Eve, and on the former served free drinks and charged for lunch, and on the latter charged for drinks and served free lunch. "Between the two they make a tidy profit."

26. Hickerson oral history, 56–57.

27. John L. Gaddis, *The Long Peace: Inquiries into the History of the Cold War*, 48–71.

28. Memorandum by Marshall of a conversation with the Swedish foreign minister, October 14, 1948, in *Foreign Relations of the United States, 1948*, vol. III, *Western Europe*, 264–66. Earlier the foreign minister of Norway, Halvard Manthey Lange, had reminded Marshall that Sweden was the only military factor in Scandinavia and could possibly develop trained ground forces of six hundred thousand men. Its navy was slightly weaker than the Soviet Navy, and although its air force was small it constituted the only air strength in the area. Sweden had a very large industrial potential. As against its potential Lange spoke of the vulnerability of Denmark and the short distance—the narrow waters—separating the latter country from Russia at Lübeck, as well as the long borders, sparse population, and general military weakness of Norway. Marshall to Lovett, September 30, 1948, in ibid., 256–57.

29. Achilles oral history, in Kaplan and Snyder, eds., *"Fingerprints on History,"* 24–26; Escott Reid, *Time of Fear and Hope: The Making of the North Atlantic*

Treaty, 1947–1949; John A. Munro and Alex I. Inglis, eds., *Mike: The Memoirs of the Right Honourable Lester B. Pearson, 1948–1957.*

30. Kaplan, *United States and NATO,* 44.

31. Francis O. Wilcox, oral history by Donald A. Ritchie, February 1, 10, March 21, April 13, June 13, 1948, 31, Truman Library; Kaplan and Snyder, eds., "*Fingerprints on History,*" 30.

32. "Senator Vandenberg, faced with a proposal to take a step into the strange and frightening postwar world, invariably began by resisting the proposal. He declared the end unattainable, the means harebrained, and the cost staggering, particularly some mysterious costs which he thought were bound to occur but which the proposer had not foreseen because of faulty preparation. This first phase, the phase of opposition, usually lasted through one meeting and sometimes longer" (Acheson, *Sketches from Life of Men I Have Known,* 126).

33. Achilles oral history, in Kaplan and Snyder, eds., "*Fingerprints on History,*" 16.

34. Bullock, *Ernest Bevin,* 680; Kaplan, *United States and NATO,* 95; Robin Edmonds, *Setting the Mould: The United States and Britain, 1945–1950,* 182–84; Howard Jones, *"A New Kind of War": America's Global Strategy and the Truman Doctrine in Greece,* 214ff.

35. Lilienthal, *Journals,* 2:632.

36. Truman to Murray, January 19, 1953. "Atomic Bomb," President's Secretary's Files, box 112, Truman papers. Also Lilienthal, *Journals,* 2:286 (January 28, 1948), 342 (May 18), 388–92 (July 21), 474–75 (February 14, 1949).

37. Borowski, *Hollow Threat,* 153–54, 169, 191.

38. For Offtackle see Etzold and Gaddis, eds., *Containment,* 324–34.

39. Rearden, *History of the Office of the Secretary of Defense,* 1:483; Kaplan, *United States and NATO,* 143.

40. Rearden, *History of the Office of the Secretary of Defense,* 1:481, 514. The definitive work on the Mutual Defense Assistance Program is Lawrence S. Kaplan, *Community of Interests: NATO and the Military Assistance Program, 1948–1951.* Title II was Greece and Turkey; III was Iran, Korea, and the Philippines. The emphasis on NATO was instructive. As Truman said to the foreign ministers on the night before the signing of the treaty, "I intend to order the Joint Chiefs of Staff to keep aid to strategically peripheral areas to the minimum. Such aid is more for internal security and psychological purposes and to warn the U.S.S.R. to keep off than for anything else. We will have to get clearly across the basic principle that any future war is going to be global, as the boys in the Kremlin well know, and that if we are strong in the decisive theaters it will keep them from striking anywhere else" (Miscellaneous Historical Documents, 626, Truman papers).

41. Rearden, *History of the Office of the Secretary of Defense,* 1:486.

42. Beaufre, *NATO and Europe,* 28–29.

43. Miscellaneous Historical Documents, 626, Truman papers. The president said that "the decisive theater is Western Europe, the only power complex sufficiently strong, combined with the U.S., to decisively redress the world power

balance and the only one which, if seized by the U.S.S.R., might render her almost impregnable."

44. Peter Foot, "The American Origins of NATO: A Study in Domestic Inhibitions and Western European Constraints," 38. Kaplan's *United States and NATO* appeared the same year as Foot completed his studies and relates a visit to Washington by the longtime exponent of a United States of Europe, Count Richard Coudenhove-Kalergi. The count was full of zeal but failed to sense the feeling among officials of the Department of State. Bohlen sent a note to Hickerson: "Coudenhove-Kalergi has been on my neck. I saw him when he was down here. You will note that he wants me to try to get him in to see the secretary. Could you let me have an estimate of his standing in Europe and whether his advocacy of European federation is taken sufficiently seriously abroad to justify recommendation that the secretary see him or is it more of a personal gambit?" (ibid., 57). The count saw Marshall for a few minutes.

Chapter Five. Truman and Korea

Originally published in *Eisenhower and Korea: The Forgotten War*, 7–20.

1. Tang Tsou, *America's Failure in China, 1941–1950*, 483.

2. U.S. Senate, Subcommittee to Investigate the Administration of the Internal Security Act and Other Internal Security Laws of the Committee of the Judiciary, Hearings, *Institute of Pacific Relations*, 5:404.

3. Steven W. Guerrier, "NSC-68 and the Truman Rearmament, 1950–1953," 197–98.

4. "Putting it bluntly, the plan was to turn the problem over to the U.N. and to get out of the way in case of trouble" (John J. Muccio, oral history by Richard D. McKinzie, 1973, 13–14, Truman Library).

5. John Edward Wilz, "The Making of Mr. Truman's War," 2.

6. William Whitney Stueck, *The Road to Confrontation: American Policy toward China and Korea, 1947–1950*, 86.

7. Sergei Goncharov, John Lewis, and Zue Litai, *Uncertain Partners: Stalin, Mao, and the Korean War*, 210.

8. Wilz, "Making of Mr. Truman's War," 9.

9. Goncharov, Lewis, and Litai, *Uncertain Partners*, 144.

10. Ibid., 145.

11. Nikita S. Khrushchev, *Khrushchev Remembers*, 368.

12. Muccio oral history, 19; Wilz, "Making of Mr. Truman's War," 11; Truman to Bess W. Truman, June 11, 1950, in Robert H. Ferrell, ed., *Off the Record: The Private Papers of Harry S. Truman*, 180; address of June 10, 1950, in *Public Papers of the Presidents: Harry S. Truman, 1950*.

13. Margaret Truman, ed., *Letters from Father: The Truman Family's Personal Correspondence*, 44.

14. Interview by William Hillman and David M. Noyes, October 21, 1959.

15. Matthew B. Ridgway, *The Korean War*, 153.

16. D. Clayton James, *The Years of MacArthur: Triumph and Disaster, 1945–1964*, 58.

17. Wilcox oral history, 118–19.

Chapter Six. Historians on Truman

Originally published in *Indiana Magazine of History* 92 (1996): 160–70.

1. Ronald J. Caridi, *The Korean War and American Politics*; Richard Dalfiume, *Desegregation of the U.S. Armed Forces: Fighting on Two Fronts, 1939–1953*; Richard O. Davies, *Housing Reform during the Truman Administration*; Robert A. Divine, *Second Chance: The Triumph of Internationalism in America during World War II*; Herbert Druks, *Harry S. Truman and the Russians, 1945–1953*; Ronald T. Farrar, *Reluctant Servant: The Story of Charles G. Ross*; Robert H. Ferrell, *George C. Marshall*; John Gimbel, *The American Occupation of Germany: Politics and the Military, 1945–1949*; Alonzo L. Hamby, *Beyond the New Deal: Harry S. Truman and American Liberalism*; Alan D. Harper, *The Politics of Loyalty: The White House and the Communist Issue, 1946–1952*; R. Alton Lee, *Truman and Taft-Hartley: A Question of Mandate*; Allen J. Matusow, *Farm Policies and Politics in the Truman Years*; Arthur F. McClure, *The Truman Administration and the Problems of Postwar Labor, 1945–1948*; Donald H. Riddle, *The Truman Committee: A Study of Congressional Responsibility*; Irwin Ross, *The Loneliest Campaign: The Truman Victory of 1948*; Richard L. Walker and George Curry, *Edward R. Stettinius, Jr., and James F. Byrnes*.

2. Gar Alperovitz, *Cold War Essays*; William C. Berman, *The Politics of Civil Rights in the Truman Administration*; Barton J. Bernstein, ed., *Politics and Policies of the Truman Administration*; Richard M. Freeland, *The Truman Doctrine and the Origins of McCarthyism: Foreign Policy, Domestic Politics, and Internal Security, 1946–1948*; Lloyd C. Gardner, *Architects of Illusion: Men and Ideas in American Foreign Policy, 1941–1949*; Thomas G. Paterson, *Soviet-American Confrontation: Postwar Reconstruction and the Origins of the Cold War*; Martin J. Sherwin, *A World Destroyed: The Atomic Bomb and the Grand Alliance*; Athan G. Theoharis, *Seeds of Repression: Harry S. Truman and the Origins of McCarthyism* and *The Yalta Myths: An Issue in U.S. Politics, 1945–1955*; Richard J. Walton, *Henry Wallace, Harry Truman, and the Cold War*; Daniel Yergin, *Shattered Peace: The Origins of the Cold War and the National Security State*.

3. Kathryn Weathersby, *Soviet Aims in Korea and the Origins of the Korean War, 1945–1950: New Evidence from Russian Archives* and "The Soviet Role in the Early Phase of the Korean War: New Documentary Evidence."

4. Barton J. Bernstein, "Seizing the Contested Terrain of Early Nuclear History" and "The Struggle over the Korean Armistice"; Bruce Cumings, *The Origins of the Korean War*; Rosemary Foot, *The Wrong War: American Policy and the Dimensions of the Korean Conflict* and *A Substitute for Victory: The Politics of Peacemaking at the Korean Armistice Talks*; Fraser J. Harbutt, *The*

Iron Curtain: Churchill, America, and the Origins of the Cold War; Frank Kofsky, *Harry S. Truman and the War Scare of 1948: A Successful Campaign to Deceive the Nation;* Melvyn P. Leffler, *A Preponderance of Power: National Security, the Truman Administration, and the Cold War;* Robert L. Messer, *The End of Alliance: James F. Byrnes, Roosevelt, Truman, and the Origins of the Cold War;* Thomas G. Paterson, *On Every Front: The Making and Unmaking of the Cold War;* Leon V. Sigal, *Fighting to the Finish: The Politics of War Termination in the United States and Japan, 1945.*

Sources

Harry S. Truman Library, Independence, Missouri

Achilles, Theodore. Oral History by Richard D. McKinzie, 1972.
Dennison, Robert L. Oral history by Jerry N. Hess, 1971.
Hickerson, John D. Oral history by Richard D. McKinzie, 1972–1973.
Hillman, William, and David M. Noyes. Interview with former president Truman, October 21, 1959.
Muccio, John J. Oral history by Richard D. McKinzie, 1973.
Truman, Harry S. Papers.
Wilcox, Francis O. Oral history by Donald A. Ritchie, 1984.

Books and Articles

Acheson, Dean. *Present at the Creation: My Years in the State Department.* New York: Norton, 1969.
———. *Sketches from Life of Men I Have Known.* New York: Harper, 1961.
Allen, Thomas B., and Norman Polmar. *Code-Name Downfall: The Secret Plan to Invade Japan—and Why Truman Dropped the Bomb.* New York: Simon and Schuster, 1995.

Alperovitz, Gar. *Atomic Diplomacy: Hiroshima and Potsdam, the Use of the Atomic Bomb and the American Confrontation with Soviet Power.* New York: Simon and Schuster, 1965.

———. *Cold War Essays.* Garden City, N.Y.: Doubleday, 1970.

———. *The Decision to Use the Atomic Bomb and the Architecture of an American Myth.* New York: Knopf, 1995.

Ambrose, Stephen E. "The Failure of a Policy Rooted in Fear." *Progressive,* November 1970.

Anderson, Terry H. *The United States, Great Britain, and the Cold War, 1944–1947.* Columbia: University of Missouri Press, 1981.

Asada, Sadao. "The Shock of the Atomic Bomb and Japan's Decision to Surrender—a Reconsideration." *Pacific Historical Review* 67 (1998): 477–512.

Barnet, Richard J. *Intervention and Revolution: America's Confrontation with Insurgent Movements around the World.* New York and Cleveland: New American Library and World, 1968.

Beaufre, André. *NATO and Europe.* New York: Knopf, 1966.

Berman, William C. *The Politics of Civil Rights in the Truman Administration.* Columbus: Ohio State University Press, 1971.

Bernstein, Barton J., ed. *Politics and Policies of the Truman Administration.* Chicago: Quadrangle, 1970.

———. "A Postwar Myth: 500,000 U.S. Lives Saved." *Bulletin of the Atomic Scientists* 42 (June–July 1986): 38–40.

———. "Seizing the Contested Terrain of Early Nuclear History." *Diplomatic History* 18 (1993): 36–72.

———. "The Struggle over the Korean Armistice." In *Child of Conflict: The Korean-American Relationship, 1943–1953,* ed. Bruce Cumings, 261–307. Seattle: University of Washington Press, 1983.

Best, Richard A., Jr. *"Co-operation with Like-Minded Peoples": British Influences on American Security Policy, 1943–1949.* Westport, Conn.: Greenwood, 1986.

Bills, Scott L., and E. Timothy Smith, eds. *The Romance of History: Essays in Honor of Lawrence S. Kaplan.* Kent: Kent State University Press, 1997.

Borowski, Harry R. *A Hollow Threat: Strategic Air Power and Containment before Korea.* Westport, Conn.: Greenwood, 1982.

Bradley, Omar N., and Clay Blair. *A General's Life: An Autobiography.* New York: Simon and Schuster, 1983.

Brodie, Bernard. *The Absolute Weapon: Atomic Power and World Order.* New York: Harcourt, Brace, 1946.

Bullock, Alan. *Ernest Bevin: Foreign Secretary, 1945–1951.* New York: Norton, 1983.

Bundschu, Henry A. *Harry S. Truman: The Missourian.* Kansas City: Kansas City Star, 1949.

Butow, Robert J. C. *Japan's Decision to Surrender.* Stanford: Stanford University Press, 1954.

Byrnes, James F. *Speaking Frankly.* New York: Harper, 1947.

Caridi, Ronald J. *The Korean War and American Politics.* Philadelphia: University of Pennsylvania Press, 1968.

Cumings, Bruce. *The Origins of the Korean War.* 2 vols. Princeton: Princeton University Press, 1981, 1990.

Dalfiume, Richard. *Desegregation of the U.S. Armed Forces: Fighting on Two Fronts, 1939–1953.* Columbia: University of Missouri Press, 1969.

Daniels, Jonathan. *The Man of Independence.* 1950. Reprint. Columbia: University of Missouri Press, 1998.

Davies, Joseph E. *Mission to Moscow.* New York: Simon and Schuster, 1941.

Davies, Richard O. *Housing Reform during the Truman Administration.* Columbia: University of Missouri Press, 1966.

Divine, Robert A. *Second Chance: The Triumph of Internationalism in America during World War II.* New York: Atheneum, 1967.

Donald, David. "Radical Historians on the Move." *New York Times Book Review,* July 19, 1970.

Donovan, Robert J. *Conflict and Crisis: The Presidency of Harry S. Truman, 1945–1948.* 1977. Reprint. Columbia: University of Missouri Press, 1996.

———. *Tumultuous Years: The Presidency of Harry S. Truman, 1949–1953.* 1982. Reprint. Columbia: University of Missouri Press, 1996.

Drea, Edward J. *In Service of the Emperor: Essays on the Imperial Japanese Army.* Lincoln: University of Nebraska Press, 1998.

———. *MacArthur's ULTRA: Codebreakers and the War against Japan, 1942–1945.* Lawrence: University Press of Kansas, 1992.

Druks, Herbert. *Harry S. Truman and the Russians, 1945–1953.* New York: Speller, 1966.

Dunar, Andrew J. *The Truman Scandals and the Politics of Morality.* Columbia: University of Missouri Press, 1984.

Edmonds, Robin. *Setting the Mould: The United States and Britain, 1945–1950.* New York: Norton, 1986.

Eisenhower and Korea: The Forgotten War. Gettysburg: Eisenhower National Historic Site, [2002].

Elsey, George M. *An Unplanned Life: A Memoir.* Columbia: University of Missouri Press, 2005.

Epstein, Klaus. "The German Problem: 1945–1950." *World Politics* 20 (1967–1968): 279–300.

Etzold, Thomas H., and John L. Gaddis, eds. *Containment: Documents on American Policy and Strategy, 1945–1950.* New York: Columbia University Press, 1978.

Farnsworth, Beatrice. *William C. Bullitt and the Soviet Union.* Bloomington: Indiana University Press, 1967.

Farrar, Ronald T. *Reluctant Servant: The Story of Charles G. Ross.* Columbia: University of Missouri Press, 1969.

Feis, Herbert. *From Trust to Terror: The Onset of the Cold War, 1945–1950.* New York: Norton, 1970.

Ferrell, Robert H. *Choosing Truman: The Chicago Convention of 1944.* Columbia: University of Missouri Press, 1994.

———. *The Dying President: Franklin D. Roosevelt, 1944–1945.* Columbia: University of Missouri Press, 1998.

———, ed. *The Eisenhower Diaries.* New York: Norton, 1981.

———, ed. *FDR's Quiet Confidant: The Autobiography of Frank C. Walker.* Niwot: University Press of Colorado, 1997.

———. *George C. Marshall.* New York: Cooper Square, 1966.

———. *Harry S. Truman: A Life.* Columbia: University of Missouri Press, 1994.

———, ed. *Harry S. Truman and the Bomb: A Documentary History.* Worland, Wyo.: High Plains, 1996.

———, ed. *Off the Record: The Private Papers of Harry S. Truman.* New York: Harper and Row, 1980.

————. *Presidential Leadership: From Woodrow Wilson to Harry S. Truman*. Columbia: University of Missouri Press, 2005.

————, ed. *Truman in the White House: The Diary of Eben A. Ayers*. Columbia: University of Missouri Press, 1991.

————, ed. "A Visit to the White House, 1947: The Diary of Vic H. Housholder." *Missouri Historical Review* 78 (1983–1984): 311–36.

Foot, Peter. "The American Origins of NATO: A Study in Domestic Inhibitions and Western European Constraints." Dissertation, University of Edinburgh, 1984.

Foot, Rosemary. *A Substitute for Victory: The Politics of Peacemaking at the Korean Armistice Talks*. Ithaca: Cornell University Press, 1990.

————. *The Wrong War: American Policy and the Dimensions of the Korean Conflict*. Ithaca: Cornell University Press, 1985.

Frank, Richard B. *Downfall: The End of the Imperial Japanese Empire*. New York: Random House, 1999.

Franklin, William M. "Zonal Boundaries and Access to Berlin." *World Politics* 16 (1963–1964): 1–31.

Freeland, Richard M. *The Truman Doctrine and the Origins of McCarthyism: Foreign Policy, Domestic Politics, and Internal Security, 1946–1948*. New York: New York University Press, 1971.

Gaddis, John L. "Domestic Influences on American Policy toward the Soviet Union, 1941–1947." Unpublished paper.

————. *The Long Peace: Inquiries into the History of the Cold War*. New York: Oxford University Press, 1987.

————. *The United States and the Origins of the Cold War: 1941–1947*. New York: Columbia University Press, 1972.

Gardner, Lloyd C. *Architects of Illusion: Men and Ideas in American Foreign Policy, 1941–1949*. Chicago: Quadrangle, 1970.

————. *Economic Aspects of New Deal Diplomacy*. Madison: University of Wisconsin Press, 1964.

Giangreco, D. M. "Casualty Projections for the U.S. Invasion of Japan, 1945–46: Planning and Policy Implications." *Journal of Military History* 61 (July 1997): 521–81.

————. "'A Score of Bloody Okinawas and Iwo Jimas': President

Truman and Casualty Estimates for the Invasion of Japan." *Pacific Historical Review* 72 (2003): 93–132.

Giangreco, D. M., and Kathryn Moore. "Half a Million Purple Hearts." *American Heritage* (December 2000–January 2001), 81–83.

Gimbel, John. *The American Occupation of Germany: Politics and the Military, 1945–1949.* Stanford: Stanford University Press, 1968.

———. "Cold War: German Front." *Maryland Historian* 2 (1971): 41–55.

Goncharov, Sergei, John Lewis, and Zue Litai. *Uncertain Partners: Stalin, Mao and the Korean War.* Stanford: Stanford University Press, 1993.

Guerrier, Steven W. "NSC-68 and the Truman Rearmament, 1950–1953." Ph.D. dissertation, University of Michigan, 1988.

Gullan, Harold I. *The Upset That Wasn't: Harry S. Truman and the Crucial Election of 1948.* Chicago: Ivan R. Dee, 1998.

Hamby, Alonzo L. *Beyond the New Deal: Harry S. Truman and American Liberalism.* New York: Columbia University Press, 1973.

———. "The Liberals, Truman, and FDR as Symbol and Myth." *Journal of American History* 56 (1969–1970): 859–67.

———. *Man of the People: A Life of Harry S. Truman.* New York: Oxford University Press, 1995.

Harbutt, Fraser J. *The Iron Curtain: Churchill, America, and the Origins of the Cold War.* New York: Oxford University Press, 1986.

Harper, Alan D. *The Politics of Loyalty: The White House and the Communist Issue, 1946–1952.* Westport, Conn.: Greenwood, 1969.

Harrington, Daniel J. *"The Air Force Can Deliver Anything!": A History of the Berlin Airlift.* Ramstein, Germany: USAFE Office of History, 1998.

Hasegawa, Tsuyoshi. *Racing the Enemy: Stalin, Truman, and the Surrender of Japan.* Cambridge: Harvard University Press, 2005.

Hathaway, Robert M. *Ambiguous Partnership: Britain and America, 1944–1947.* New York: Columbia University Press, 1981.

Hechler, Ken. *Working with Truman: A Personal Memoir.* 1982. Reprint. Columbia: University of Missouri Press, 1996.

Helm, William P. *Harry Truman: A Political Biography.* New York: Duell, Sloan and Pearce, 1947.

Herken, Gregg. *The Winning Weapon: The Atomic Bomb in the Cold War, 1945–1950.* New York: Knopf, 1980.

Herring, George C., Jr. "Lend Lease to Russia and the Origins of the Cold War, 1944–1945." *Journal of American History* 56 (1969–1970): 93–114.

Herschler, David. "Retreat in Germany: The Decision to Withdraw Anglo-American Forces from the Soviet Occupation Zone, 1945." Ph.D. dissertation, Indiana University, 1977.

James, D. Clayton. *The Years of MacArthur: Triumph and Disaster, 1945–1964.* Boston: Houghton Mifflin, 1985.

Jones, Howard. *"A New Kind of War": America's Global Strategy and the Truman Doctrine in Greece.* New York: Oxford University Press, 1989.

Kaplan, Lawrence S., ed. *American Historians and the Atlantic Alliance.* Kent: Kent State University Press, 1991.

———. *Community of Interests: NATO and the Military Assistance Program, 1948–1951.* Washington, D.C.: Government Printing Office, 1980.

———. *The United States and NATO: The Formative Years.* Lexington: University Press of Kentucky, 1984.

Kaplan, Lawrence S., and Sidney R. Snyder, eds. *"Fingerprints on History": The NATO Memoirs of Theodore C. Achilles.* Kent, Ohio: Lemnitzer Center, 1992.

Kemper, R. Crosby III, ed. *Winston Churchill: Resolution, Defiance, Magnanimity, Good Will.* Columbia: University of Missouri Press, 1996.

Khrushchev, Nikita S. *Khrushchev Remembers.* Boston: Little, Brown, 1970.

Kirkendall, Richard S., ed. *Harry's Farewell: Interpreting and Teaching the Truman Presidency.* Columbia: University of Missouri Press, 2004.

———, ed. *The Truman Period as a Research Field: A Reappraisal, 1972.* Columbia: University of Missouri Press, 1974.

Kofsky, Frank. *Harry S. Truman and the War Scare of 1948: A Successful Campaign to Deceive the Nation.* New York: St. Martin's, 1993.

Kolko, Gabriel. *The Politics of War: The World and United States Foreign Policy, 1943–1945.* New York: Random House, 1968.

LaFeber, Walter. *America, Russia, and the Cold War.* 2d ed. New York: Wiley, 1972.

———. *The New Empire: An Interpretation of American Expansion, 1860–1898.* Ithaca: Cornell University Press, 1963.

————, ed. *Origins of the Cold War, 1941–1947: Documents and Problems.* New York: Wiley, 1971.

Lee, R. Alton. *Truman and Taft-Hartley: A Question of Mandate.* Lexington: University of Kentucky Press, 1966.

Leffler, Milvyn P. "The American Conception of National Security and the Beginnings of the Cold War, 1945–1948." *American Historical Review* 89 (April 1984): 346–81.

————. *A Preponderance of Power: National Security, the Truman Administration, and the Cold War.* Stanford: Stanford University Press, 1991.

Lilienthal, David E. *The Journals of David E. Lilienthal.* Vol. 2. New York: Harper and Row, 1964.

Lukacs, John. *Churchill: Visionary, Statesman, Historian.* New Haven: Yale University Press, 2002.

————. *The End of the Twentieth Century and the End of the Modern Age.* New York: Ticknor and Fields, 1993.

————. *A New History of the Cold War.* Garden City, N.Y.: Doubleday, 1966.

————. *A New Republic: A History of the United States in the Twentieth Century.* New Haven: Yale University Press, 2004.

————. *Year Zero.* Garden City, N.Y.: Doubleday, 1978.

MacEachin, Douglas J. *The Final Months of the War with Japan: Signals Intelligence, Invasion Planning, and the A-Bomb Decision.* Washington, D.C.: Central Intelligence Agency, Center for the Study of Intelligence, 1998.

Maddox, Robert J. "Cold War Revisionism: Abusing History." *Freedom at Issue* (September–October 1972): 3–6, 16–19.

————. *The New Left and the Origins of the Cold War.* Princeton: Princeton University Press, 1973.

————. *Weapons for Victory: The Hiroshima Decision Fifty Years Later.* Columbia: University of Missouri Press, 1995.

Maier, Charles S. "Revisionism and the Interpretation of Cold War Origins." *Perspectives in American History* 4 (1970): 313–47.

Matusow, Allen J. *Farm Policies and Politics in the Truman Years.* Cambridge: Harvard University Press, 1967.

McClure, Arthur F. *The Truman Administration and the Problem of*

Postwar Labor, 1945–1948. Rutherford, N.J.: Fairleigh Dickinson University Press, 1969.

McCoy, Donald R. *The Presidency of Harry S. Truman.* Lawrence: University Press of Kansas, 1984.

McCullough, David. *Truman.* New York: Simon and Schuster, 1992.

Messer, Robert L. *The End of an Alliance: James F. Byrnes, Roosevelt, Truman, and the Origins of the Cold War.* Chapel Hill: University of North Carolina Press, 1982.

Miller, Merle. *Plain Speaking: An Oral Biography of Harry S. Truman.* New York: Berkley, 1973.

Miller, Richard Lawrence. *Truman: The Rise to Power.* New York: McGraw-Hill, 1986.

Munro, John A., and Alex I. Inglis, eds. *Mike: The Memoirs of the Right Honourable Lester B. Pearson, 1948–1957.* New York: Quadrangle, 1973.

Newman, Robert P. *Enola Gay and the Court of History.* New York: Lang, 2004.

———. *Truman and the Hiroshima Cult.* East Lansing: Michigan State University Press, 1995.

Newton, Verne W. *The Cambridge Spies: The Untold Story of Maclean, Philby, and Burgess in America.* Lanham, Md.: Madison, 1991.

Offner, Arnold A. *Another Such Victory: President Truman and the Cold War, 1945–1953.* Stanford: Stanford University Press, 2002.

Paterson, Thomas G. "The Abortive American Loan to Russia and the Origins of the Cold War, 1943–1946." *Journal of American History* 56 (1969–1970): 70–92.

———, ed. *Cold War Critics: Alternatives to American Foreign Policy in the Truman Years.* Chicago: Quadrangle, 1971.

———. *On Every Front: The Making and Unmaking of the Cold War.* Rev. ed. New York: Norton, 1992.

———, ed. *The Origins of the Cold War.* Lexington, Mass.: Heath, 1970. 2nd ed., 1974.

———. *Soviet-American Confrontation: Postwar Reconstruction and the Origins of the Cold War.* Baltimore: Johns Hopkins University Press, 1973.

Paterson, Thomas G., and Les Adler. "Red Fascism: The Merger of Nazi

Germany and Soviet Russia in the American Image of Totalitarianism, 1930's-1950's." *American Historical Review* 75 (1969–1970):
1046–64.

Pemberton, William E. *Harry S. Truman: Fair Dealer and Cold Warrior.*
Boston: Twayne, 1989.

Phillips, Cabell. *The Truman Presidency: The History of a Triumphant
Succession.* New York: Macmillan, 1966.

Poen, Monte M. *Harry S. Truman versus the Medical Lobby: The Genesis
of Medicare.* Columbia: University of Missouri Press, 1979.

———, ed. *Letters Home by Harry Truman.* 1984. Reprint. Columbia:
University of Missouri Press, 2003.

———, ed. *Strictly Personal and Confidential: The Letters Harry Truman
Never Mailed.* 1982. Reprint. Columbia: University of Missouri
Press, 1999.

Public Papers of the Presidents: Harry S. Truman, 1950. Washington,
D.C.: Government Printing Office, 1951.

Rearden, Steven L. *History of the Office of the Secretary of Defense.* Vol. 1.
The Formative Years, 1947–1950. Washington, D.C.: Office of the
Secretary of Defense, 1984.

Reid, Escott. *Time of Fear and Hope: The Making of the North Atlantic
Treaty, 1947–1949.* Toronto: McClelland and Stewart, 1977.

Riddle, Donald H. *The Truman Committee: A Study of Congressional
Responsibility.* New Brunswick, N.J.: Rutgers University Press, 1964.

Ridgway, Matthew B. *The Korean War.* Garden City, N.Y.: Doubleday,
1967.

Rose, Lisle A. *After Yalta.* New York: Scribner's, 1973.

Rosenberg, David Alan. "American Atomic Strategy and the Hydrogen
Bomb Decision." *Journal of American History* 66 (1978–1979):
62–87.

———. "U.S. Nuclear Stockpile 1945 to 1950." *Bulletin of the Atomic
Scientists* 35 (1982): 25–31.

Ross, Irwin. *The Loneliest Campaign: The Truman Victory of 1948.* New
York: New American Library, 1968.

Rostow, Walt W. *The Stages of Economic Growth: A Non-Communist
Manifesto.* New York: Cambridge University Press, 1962.

Schlesinger, Arthur M., Jr. "Origins of the Cold War." *Foreign Affairs* 46 (1967–1968): 22–52.

Sherwin, Martin J. *A World Destroyed: The Atomic Bomb and the Grand Alliance.* New York: Knopf, 1975.

Sigal, Leon V. *Fighting to the Finish: The Politics of War Termination in the United States and Japan, 1945.* Ithaca: Cornell University Press, 1988.

Snell, John L. "The Cold War: Four Contemporary Appraisals." *American Historical Review* 68 (1962–1963): 69–75.

Steel, Ronald. *Imperialists and Other Heroes: A Chronicle of the American Empire.* New York: Random House, 1971.

Steinberg, Alfred. *The Man from Missouri: The Life and Times of Harry S. Truman.* New York: Putnam, 1962.

Stueck, William Whitney. *Rethinking the Korean War: A New Diplomatic and Strategic History.* Princeton: Princeton University Press, 2002.

———. *The Road to Confrontation: American Policy toward China and Korea, 1947–1950.* Chapel Hill: University of North Carolina Press, 1981.

Tansill, Charles C. *Back Door to War: The Roosevelt Foreign Policy, 1933–1941.* Chicago: Regnery, 1952.

Theoharis, Athan G. *Seeds of Repression: Harry S. Truman and the Origins of McCarthyism.* Chicago: Quadrangle, 1971.

———. *The Yalta Myths: An Issue in U.S. Politics, 1945–1955.* Columbia: University of Missouri Press, 1970.

Trevor-Roper, H. R. "The Lost Moments of History." *New York Review of Books* 27 (October 1988).

Truman, Harry S. *Memoirs.* 2 vols. Garden City, N.Y.: Doubleday, 1955, 1956.

Truman, Margaret. *Bess W. Truman.* New York: Macmillan, 1986.

———. *Harry S. Truman.* New York: Morrow, 1973.

———, ed. *Letters from Father: The Truman Family's Personal Correspondence.* New York: Arbor House, 1981.

———. *Souvenir: Margaret Truman's Own Story.* New York: McGraw-Hill, 1956.

————, ed. *Where the Buck Stops: The Personal and Private Writings of Harry S. Truman.* New York: Warner, 1989.

Tsou, Tang. *America's Failure in China, 1941–1950.* Chicago: University of Chicago Press, 1963.

————. "Civil Strife and Armed Intervention: Marshall's China Policy." *Orbis* 6 (1962).

Tucker, Robert C. "The Cold War in Stalin's Time: What the New Sources Reveal." *Diplomatic History* 21 (1997): 273–83.

Ulam, Adam B. *The Rivals: America and Russia since World War II.* New York: Viking, 1971.

Unger, Irwin. "The New Left and American History: Some Recent Trends in United States Historiography." *American Historical Review* 72 (1966–1967).

U.S. Department of State. *Foreign Relations of the United States: The Conference of Berlin, 1945.* 2 vols. Washington, D.C.: Government Printing Office, 1960.

————. *Foreign Relations of the United States, 1946,* vol. VII, *The Near East and Africa.* Washington, D.C.: Government Printing Office, 1969.

————. *Foreign Relations of the United States, 1948,* vol. III, *Western Europe.* Washington, D.C.: Government Printing Office, 1974.

U.S. Senate. Committee on Foreign Relations. *Documents on Germany, 1944–1970.* 92nd Cong., 1st sess. Washington, D.C.: Government Printing Office, 1971.

————. Subcommittee to Investigate the Administration of the Internal Security Act and Other Internal Security Laws of the Committee of the Judiciary. Hearings. *Institute of Pacific Relations.* 82nd Cong., 1st sess. 15 vols. Washington, D.C.: Government Printing Office, 1951–1953.

Walker, J. Samuel. *Prompt and Utter Destruction: Truman and the Use of Atomic Bombs against Japan.* Chapel Hill: University of North Carolina Press, 1997.

Walker, Richard L., and George Curry. *Edward R. Stettinius, Jr., and James F. Byrnes.* New York: Cooper Square, 1965.

Walton, Richard J. *Henry Wallace, Harry Truman, and the Cold War.* New York: Viking, 1976.

Weathersby, Kathryn. *Soviet Aims in Korea and the Origins of the Korean War, 1945–1950: New Evidence from Russian Archives.* Washington, D.C.: Woodrow Wilson International Center for Scholars, 1993.
———. "The Soviet Role in the Early Phase of the Korean War: New Documentary Evidence." *Journal of American-East Asian Relations* 2 (winter 1993): 425–58.

White, Theodore H. *Fire in the Ashes: Europe in Mid-Century.* New York: Sloane, 1953.

Williamson, Samuel R., Jr., and Steven L. Rearden. *The Origins of U.S. Nuclear Strategy, 1945–1953.* New York: St. Martin's, 1993.

Wilz, John Edward. "The Making of Mr. Truman's War." Manuscript. Courtesy of the author.

Woods, Randall B. *A Changing of the Guard: Anglo-American Relations, 1941–1946.* Chapel Hill: University of North Carolina Press, 1990.
———. *Fulbright: A Biography.* New York: Cambridge University Press, 1995.

Woods, Randall B., and Howard Jones. *Dawning of the Cold War: The United States' Quest for Order.* Athens: University of Georgia Press, 1991.

Yergin, Daniel. *Shattered Peace: The Origins of the Cold War and the National Security State.* Boston: Houghton Mifflin, 1977.

Index